EUROPE

EUROPE

The State of the Union

ANAND MENON

Atlantic Books
LONDON

First published in Great Britain in 2008 by Atlantic Books,
an imprint of Grove Atlantic Ltd.

9 8 7 6 5 4 3 2 1

A CIP catalogue record for this book is available from
the British Library.

ISBN: 978 1 84354 479 1

Design and typsetting in Perpetua by Lindsay Nash
Printed in Great Britain by MPG Books Ltd, Bodmin, Cornwall

Atlantic Books
An imprint of Grove Atlantic Ltd
Ormond House
26–27 Boswell Street
London WC1N 3JZ

www.groveatlantic.co.uk

CONTENTS

ACKNOWLEDGEMENTS

After some fifteen years spent teaching and learning about European integration, my intellectual debts are numerous and profound; too numerous and profound, in fact, to acknowledge in detail here. I no longer remember, moreover, where I first heard certain of the ideas expressed in the pages that follow, and am sure that several of those I now believe to be my own were in fact expressed by someone else at some conference or workshop. So let me simply express my gratitude to all those – policy makers, journalists, colleagues, teachers and even (on rare occasions) students – whose wisdom informs the pages that follow.

Particular thanks are due to several friends and family members who have contributed beyond the call of duty. Hussein Kassim and I have spent far too long talking about the European Union, for which I owe him both my thanks and my apologies. Julian Cooper, Archana, Deepika and Mohan all provided useful feedback on what follows. Nigel was surprisingly and reassuringly positive. Colm took time out of an unbelievably hectic schedule to read and comment on the whole manuscript. Andy Charlton read the first page and didn't like it. Ian Anderson, Julia De Clerck Sachsse and Chris Hanretty provided invaluable research assistance. Dionyssis, Jack Hayward and Dan read the whole thing and provided, as they always do, detailed, perceptive and helpful comments and advice. Dan did so despite disagreeing with much of what follows.

Toby Mundy of Atlantic Books was unbelievably encouraging throughout the seemingly endless writing process. I'm not convinced the book justifies the faith he continually expressed in me, but I am grateful for it nevertheless. In contrast, the barely suppressed boredom of Heidi, Paul, Philippa, Ian, Louise and Goose served as a salutary reminder that I won't be able to retire on its proceeds. Emma's enthusiasm was puzzling, though much appreciated. Zoe bore the brunt of my increasing irascibility – doubly unfairly having previously provided very helpful comments.

Samuel, meanwhile, deserves recognition, if not thanks, for his supreme indifference. I am dedicating this book to him in the hope, rather than the expectation, that, one day, he'll have more to say than 'whatever' when someone mentions the EU.

Finally, my dad fell seriously ill while I was finishing this manuscript. Happily, he now seems well on the road to recovery but his illness promoted me to realize, in a way I had previously failed to, how much I owe my parents. Thank you hardly begins to scratch the surface of that debt. Nevertheless, my heartfelt thanks to you both.

EUROPE FOR THE EXASPERATED

F iftieth birthdays are a time for reflection, not always positive. Fifty years ago, in January 1958, the European Economic Community (EEC) was born. Some fifty years later, 'Europe' was described by an *Economist* leading article as being in the throes of a 'mid-life crisis'.[1]

All of which is curious, and for several reasons. The first couple are a little pedantic, but I do want to get them off my chest. For one thing, people are far too quick to associate the notions of 'Europe' and 'European Union' (EU). Quite apart from annoying the Norwegians, Russians, Swiss, Turks and Ukrainians, among others, this has, as we shall see, the effect of making us expect more of the EU than we have any right to.

Second, the European Union itself is actually almost fifteen, not fifty. It came into being in November 1993 and includes within it the EC that dates back to the 1958 Treaty of Rome.[2] I realize few people care, but fiftieth-birthday celebrations for a fifteen-year-old tell us something about the ignorance surrounding European integration.

Third, the numerous parties and receptions held in April 2007 commemorated not the coming into being of the EEC but the signing of the treaty that led to its creation. That didn't make them any less enjoyable. And, besides, I'd never been to a conception party before. Yet the timing was wholly indicative of a prevailing and unhealthy obsession with EU institutions and treaties rather than EU actions.

Finally, while most people dread their mid-life crises, the Union had every reason to appreciate news of its own. After all, in 1982, the selfsame *Economist* had commemorated the EC's twenty-fifth birthday with a cover picture of a tombstone bearing the inscription 'EC RIP'.

Ignorance, indifference, and wildly varying assessments — all are characteristic of popular attitudes towards the EU. What is the *point* of European integration? What does the EU *do*? What, if anything, has it *achieved*? Few people, it seems, could provide answers to these questions.

The lack of interest stems, in part at least, from boredom. Much of what the European Union does is dull. After some fifteen years of lecturing to comatose students about it, I can attest to this. The EU's core functions are regulation, the negotiation of trade agreements, the setting of interest rates and the like. And, more often than not, the issues at stake are technical and apparently trivial. In 2001, for instance, the Union painstakingly produced a piece of legislation defining fruit (those with an interest, fear not, we return to this later). Moreover, its foreign policy is 'soft', its institutions are remote, and its greatest crisis involved the boycotting of committee meetings. Even its scandals are dull and tend to be prompted by auditors' reports. Admittedly, a former French Prime Minister, Édith Cresson, gave us some grounds for optimism when, as European Commissioner, she was accused of nepotism towards her octogenarian dentist. This, sadly, involved the provision of an office and salary, rather than anything more exciting.

A further reason for incomprehension is the Union's uniqueness. Most people, whether they care to admit it or not, judge themselves in comparison to others, particularly, no doubt, on those landmark birthdays. Yet what to compare the EU with? An international organization like the UN? A federal state like the US? A free trade association like NAFTA? As it happens, none is an ideal comparator, though comparison with the UN probably works best.

The point is that the Union fails neatly to fit into any of the conceptual boxes we have created to discuss political phenomena, which in turn renders assessment of it difficult. At once its most intriguing and infuriating characteristic is that it is interesting as much for what it is not as for what it is. It passes laws but has no government; it has a defence policy but no army; it dabbles in social policy but not in matters pertaining to the welfare state; it has a currency but little or no access to the other levers of economic policy.

Assessing the Union, therefore, requires an understanding of how it works and what it does. Unfortunately, it remains one of the least well-understood political systems in the world, and this in part is because of the nature of politics within it. Unlike federal states, the Union is not populated by political parties devoted to the capture of high office at its centre. The reasons for this are examined later, but for now the important point is that, whatever their shortcomings, political parties play a crucial educational role in political debates. Because they compete for election, they are compelled to explain the issues at hand to their electorates. Because the Union rarely figures as an issue in national elections, and European Parliament elections are dominated by national debates about national politics, parties do not play this role for it.

Public discussion of the Union, in other words, is sporadic at best. Consequently, such debates as there are tend to be dominated by academics and commentators, all of whom revel in dreaming up ever more abstract and pretentious formulations to describe it. The interested layperson is thus confronted with a morass of obfuscatory jargon including gems such as 'absorption capacity', 'the community method', 'comitology', 'supranationalism', 'bicycle theories' and the like. Politicians are little better. Rather than explaining the Union to their citizens, they conspire (admittedly for good reasons, as we see in chapter 1) in making it seem both opaque and remote.

As if this were not enough, the Union is fiendishly complex – making accuracy and stimulation difficult to reconcile. The combination of complexity and uniqueness is problematic in a world where politics is discussed in soundbites. The upshot is a highly polarized dialogue of the deaf. 'Sophistication and modulation, nuance and understatement, have not been prominent in the language of the EU's detractors,' noted Chris Patten.[3] He was right, except that the same can equally be said of the Union's admirers. Partly because of the difficulties involved in describing it as it is, both proponents and opponents of integration describe it in terms of what they wish, or fear, to see, rather than what actually is. Whether describing a threatening super-state or a welcome replacement for the nation state, Europhiles and Europhobes alike portray a fictional future disguised as fact.

So, the purpose of this book is to try to assess what the Union is and does, rather than what it might, or should, do or become. It steers a course between the excesses of the Europhiles and Eurosceptics. Unlike the latter, it argues that the EU is both a necessary and a generally effective tool of the member states. In contrast to the former, it does not turn this appreciation into an uncritical acceptance of everything the Union does. There are, as the subsequent pages illustrate all too clearly, some things it should not attempt, and some things it attempts unsuccessfully. I am on occasion highly sceptical – particularly as regards attempts to expand the competence of the Union too far beyond its original focus on the creation of a European market. Yet I am also broadly supportive of what I see as a unique process in political history whose achievements to date are too infrequently appreciated by both sceptics and Europhiles alike.

At the time of writing, there is fevered speculation as to whether or not referenda will be called to ratify the Reform

Treaty currently being negotiated by the twenty-seven governments. Personally, I believe the Union is a tool of, rather than a putative replacement for, its member states. Its very nature condemns it to being the object of, at best, public indifference. Consequently, referenda on technical and virtually unreadable legal texts are an inappropriate way of deciding on its operating rules. Which is not to say, of course, that they will not be held. Given that people vote on the basis of their views of the Union rather than their critical appraisal of any treaty text, it is important that they grasp what the EU is, and what it does.

The chapters to come address in turn the following questions: why do states bother to create institutions like the EU? Why, having done so, are politicians so reluctant to explain them to their populations? How has European integration developed since its inception in the 1950s? How does the contemporary European Union work? What exactly does it do, and how well does it carry out these tasks? And, finally, what is the state of the European Union today?

The response to this final question is intimately linked to, and emerges from, responses to the preceding ones. Given its fragility, its dependence on its member states, its lack of resources, and the hugely complex and sensitive nature of what it does, the Union stands as a triumph of interstate cooperation. Certainly, it is far from perfect, and its functioning – particularly its relationship with the member states – could be improved upon in several ways. Moreover, its nature places limits upon what it could, or should, aspire to do, limits which, if ignored, could challenge the undertaking as a whole. The European Union, however, is something that Europeans and their political leaders should appreciate far more than they do. In order to do so (and in order to vote on its future), they need to understand it.

1

THE PARADOX OF INTEGRATION

Why do states create institutions like the European Union? What purpose do they serve? After all, both the European states themselves throughout most of their history and other states in other parts of the contemporary world seem to get along perfectly well without them. And if there is a purpose to the Union, why do so few people know what it is?

My intention in this chapter is to set out a generic explanation as to why states create international institutions, and why politicians prove so inadequate at explaining these reasons. Being generic, it is somewhat abstract, leaving it to subsequent chapters to fill out the details as to what precisely the EU is and does, and how it works in practice. Thus, as chapter 2 illustrates, each member state sees a slightly different rationale for European integration; and, as I show in chapter 3, the Union is a unique kind of international institution. What follows is simply intended to set the context. Chapter 7 returns to some of the broad themes raised here in the light of the intervening discussion.

Simply put, contemporary European states need international institutions to ensure their own effectiveness. The EU is a response to the changing nature of politics in twenty-first-century Europe. That it is rarely discussed in these terms is attributable to many factors, not least an uninformed and uninformative media and an indifferent public willing to read sensationalist headlines but little else. It is also, however, a function of the attitudes of national politicians. The structure of national politics and the incentives it produces tend to condemn them to talk up their own capacities at the expense of those institutions specifically designed to reinforce them. There are, in the cut-throat world of competitive democratic politics, fewer prizes for accuracy than for self-promotion. Herein lies the paradox of integration, as a result of which the European Union remains profoundly necessary yet equally profoundly misunderstood.

This chapter explores the paradox. Beginning with an explanation of how the expanding links between states make the creation of international institutions seem ever more attractive, it goes on to explain why it is that political incentives militate against clear explanations of this attractiveness.

★

Government, as we understand it, is a relatively new phenomenon. As recently as the nineteenth century, its role was restricted to merely a few core functions. To all intents and purposes, 'nobody was governed before the later nineteenth century.'[1] All this began to change as a consequence of the technological advances associated with industrialization, which allowed for a massive increase in the size and effectiveness of bureaucracy. In Britain, a civil service which had numbered 27,000 in 1821 had reached 80,000 by 1881, and 1,056,000 (central government only) in 1985.[2] And a larger bureaucracy paved the way for a concomitant expansion of state ambitions, hitherto restricted by limited capabilities. Government expenditure, only 14 per cent of GNP in 1900, had reached 36 per cent by the 1950s.[3]

Moreover, while such expenditures were once devoted only to three major priorities – defence, servicing the national debt (paying for previous wars) and the costs of governmental administration – by the end of the Second World War this had changed. The dominant conception of the role of government was that it made 'the promise… to take full responsibility for the economic welfare of a given population through the deft exercise of the power of its state'.[4] Government now, rightly or wrongly, has something to say about everything from how we care for our children to what we eat. More importantly for our purposes, growing involvement in economic issues focused popular attention on the state's role in delivering prosperity. By the 1970s, MORI was finding that the economy was the number one priority in the minds of the population.[5]

This perception of governments as key providers of economic goods confronted them with the need to reconcile rising demands with limited resources. Changing tastes and increasing desires meant that purely national provision of economic goods was no longer enough. An obvious solution was to seek answers abroad. Trade held out the promise of increasing economic provision to ever more expectant populations, allowing states to secure from others what it was not possible for them to supply alone.

Steep rises in international trade, and indeed in cross-border activity of all kinds, however, made governments increasingly reliant on each other. Their interdependence made states sensitive to the actions of other states. It affects France when Russia turns off the tap on its gas pipelines; and the British suffer when French air traffic controllers go on strike (as they invariably do).

Compounding the effects of interdependence has been the impact of what is referred to (and there are almost as many definitions as there are accounts) as 'globalization'. The mobility of capital, transferable instantaneously by computer terminals across the globe; the attendant power of financial markets (which, in 2004, were achieving an average daily turnover of $1.9 trillion in the foreign exchange markets); the influence of global corporations that can hold governments to ransom by brandishing the threat of relocation; and the increasing ease of global communications and transport have combined to challenge established patterns of national politics.

Technology has also served to transform even traditional economic sectors. Industries that were once seen as natural monopolies, such as telecommunications and energy supply, have been revolutionized. Electricity is now freely supplied across borders, telecoms operators in one country provide domestic calling facilities in another and predatory foreign firms buy up utilities giants. We live in a world in which the FA Cup, if not sponsored by a French insurance giant, gets funding from a German energy monopoly.

Furious debates rage about the degree to which economic forces constrain states. Yet it is not necessary to accept that globalization spells the end of the state to understand the pressures it places upon it. The web of interdependencies in which states find themselves, compounded by their growing openness to international forces, places significant new constraints upon them.

The problem with this is the sheer uncertainty inherent in dependence upon others. This provides powerful incentives for governments to try to impose a degree of stability and predictability on these relations. Cooperation can potentially achieve this. However, ensuring cooperation is never easy. Be it a marriage, a partnership or the relationship between a Prime Minister and a Chancellor, signatories to any agreement face strong incentives to let the others do all the work (free-ride), or simply ignore their obligations (cheat). Such problems are all the more acute in international, as opposed to domestic, politics. Within states, individuals have recourse to the law, and to authorities created to enforce it. Nothing comparable exists for politics between states. The international realm is an anarchic one. Consequently, states are notoriously distrustful of each other, and obsessed, even in the face of overwhelming incentives to cooperate, with the possibility of their partners not playing fair.

The Swiss philosopher Jean-Jacques Rousseau used an analogy with a stag hunt in his *Discourse on Inequality* to illustrate the problem. A group of hungry men set out to hunt a stag, knowing that it would feed all of them, while each would be satisfied with a hare. One of them sees a hare, grabs it, and runs off with his prize. As a consequence, it becomes much harder for those remaining to run down the stag. Because no one in international politics knows when another will run off, each has an incentive to do so first. As Rousseau put it, 'if a hare happened to pass within reach of one of them, we cannot doubt that he would have gone off in pursuit of it without scruple.'

Rousseau's solution to the fruitless quest for cooperation was a world of autonomous, self-sufficient states with only limited dealings with each other. Yet this is hardly a realistic proposition at the start of the twenty-first century. An alternative is to use international institutions. Think of stags again. Assume the hunters appointed a village elder to oversee the hunt – a Hunt Tsar, if you like. This immediately changes the nature of the enterprise. If the hunt were a one-off affair, I might well be tempted to kill the hare. The appointment of an overseer implies it might be more regular, and, knowing I'd have to go hunting again with the same group of men, I might think twice before letting them down. The Tsar could also be charged with checking whether hunters run after hares and, if they do so, with imposing penalties on them (perhaps even confiscating the hare).

The point is that, in the presence of an impartial overseer, the incentives facing the hunters change. And such is also the potential role of institutions in international politics. By creating them, states are in effect not only implying that cooperation will last into the future, but also setting up mechanisms to deal with potential cheating or free-riding.

★

International institutions can take many forms, ranging from loose, information-sharing arrangements, such as the Organization for Economic Cooperation and Development (OECD) to complex and relatively intrusive structures like the World Trade Organization. A crucial difference between them is their independence from the member states that created them. The Americans wield disproportionate influence over the World Bank because they pay most into its budget. The Secretariat General of the United Nations is an institution intended to foster effective interstate cooperation, but it is crucially constrained by the Security Council. The European Union is, in contrast, remarkably independent in many ways. Why, then, would states opt for this model?

Part of the answer lies, as explained in the next chapter, in historical contingency. The conditions under which European integration came into being largely explain its unique character. Yet the fact that the member states have maintained much of the model adopted in the 1950s indicates that it is also explicable in terms of their need to ensure effective cooperation.

If a group of highly interdependent countries seek to achieve stability in their relations, the institutions created to accomplish this need to enjoy independence from them. Failing this, they will not be trusted to carry out their tasks impartially. One need only look at the reactions of many Third World states to the strictures of the World Bank to realize what accusations of domination by any one country can do to trust.

Such was the need felt to ensure stable economic interactions between the West European states that the institutions of the EU enjoy far more formal autonomy from them than is the case in any other international organization. The European Commission, European Court of Justice and European Central Bank all have their independence from their member state creators formally enshrined in the treaties that created them. The theory is that this will ensure that they are trusted and allow them to represent the general – European – interest rather than those of any particular state or group of states.

Independence is also explicable in terms of the functions these institutions perform. It has become increasingly commonplace for the management of certain economic functions *within* states to be entrusted to independent bodies. This is far from novel. Samy Finer's magisterial study of the history of government illustrates how European states became constitutionalized from the early nineteenth century. This implied a desire to insulate certain aspects of public policy, and in particular certain core individual and group rights, from the control of the majority. Thus, liberal democracy is 'qualified democracy', in that the 'ultimate right of the majority to have its way is conceded, but that way is made as rough as possible'.[6] The entrenchment of basic rights and liberties necessitated the delegation of judicial powers to independent judges. And this tendency has spread in recent years as courts increasingly do not simply adjudicate rights but define and redefine them.

Governments, in other words, have for years shared some of the tasks of governing with other, non-elected bodies. And as politics and policy have become more complex, the tendency to do so has become ever more widespread, in terms both of the range of issues covered and of the autonomy granted to the relevant institutions. One reason for this is expertise. It is now often assumed that experts can make decisions on highly technical matters – such as medical safety or food standards – more effectively than elected politicians. This is not to say that politicians would be incapable of making reasoned judgements about technical matters – they do, after all, continue to control taxation. Nor is it to claim that science is necessarily truly 'objective'. The debates over BSE, which saw continental European veterinary experts ranged against their British counterparts, illustrated all too clearly the link between national cultures and traditions and scientific 'fact'. Yet 'delegation', or the process by which tasks are entrusted to formally independent actors, does represent a means of trying to ensure efficient decision making in highly specialist areas where the alternative would be, at a minimum, to impose substantial time costs on elected politicians.

A further reason for reliance on unelected expertise is distrust of politics or, more specifically, a fear of political short-termism. Politicians, understandably enough, always have an eye on the next election. Consequently, they face incentives to take decisions that provide short-term benefits, even if these imply long-term costs (what economists refer to as the 'time inconsistency problem'). Yet in, say, monetary or competition policy, these are hardly criteria designed to bring about optimal outcomes. Pre-election interest rate cuts are paid for in terms of inflation and higher rates after the vote. Politically motivated competition policy decisions are not a basis for the creation of an efficient market. Making central banks and competition authorities independent of government is thus seen as a logical way of addressing the problems inherent in systems of democratic government prone to electioneering and clientelism.

As a consequence of these various pressures and incentives, European democracies have taken to entrusting a wide variety of functions to agencies, boards, trusts and tribunals. A 2004 survey by the British Cabinet Office revealed the existence of 839 'public bodies', of which more than a quarter are 'executive'. Indeed, following the intelligence failures in the lead-up to the 2003 Gulf War, there were those who suggested that intelligence analysis should be carried out by autonomous executive agencies independent of the government and civil service.[7]

The ability of governments directly to shape policy is thus reduced. Interest rates can no longer be wielded as a

political tool. Private ownership and independent regulation of previously state-owned industries reduce the ability
of politicians to use these for their own electoral purposes.
And the reasons which justify the independence of the
various boards, trusts and agencies *within* European states
can be applied to those institutions created to regulate
interactions *between* them. The European Commission,
European Court of Justice and European Central Bank are,
like their domestic counterparts, independent institutions
entrusted with certain specific functions. Independence
from the member states is intended to facilitate both their
task of acting as impartial referees of cooperation and their
involvement in making substantive policy decisions.

Viewed in this light, European integration does not represent a break with 'normal' political practice but, rather, a
rational response to the implications of the changing nature
of government. It can be seen, in other words, as an attempt
on the part of the member states to deal with the growing
messiness and complexity of politics. Addressing the
transnational issues spawned by growing interdependence
requires a transnational framework. Ensuring effective
cooperation and economic management militates in favour
of independent institutions.

It is not, of course, quite as simple as this. The potential
cost of institution building is that governments find themselves constrained by the new rules to which they have
signed up. Because these emerge from a process of bargaining, they are unlikely perfectly to reflect the preferences of
any individual participant. The ultimate trade-off, therefore,

is between the costs of complying with rules and the potential benefits of cooperation.

It gets messier still. Institutions are not simply about rational calculations of the costs and benefits of individual versus collective action. After all, if they were, nation states themselves would not exist – being frequently too small to allow for the effective unilateral accomplishment of key tasks. The question of what to entrust to international institutions is a matter of politics. Nation states are more than simply the units into which international politics is divided. They are communities whose populations feel a certain loyalty towards them. Even given an overwhelming rationale for collective action, some issues may be considered simply too important to entrust to others. Control over decisions relating to matters of war and peace provides one obvious example.

In the case of European integration, unusually independent institutions were acceptable partly because the EC from the start dealt largely with matters of trade and regulation. Even willingness to cooperate in these areas has its limits, however, as we shall see. Cooperative undertakings touching on core aspects of national sovereignty or national identity, meanwhile, meet stiff resistance, whatever the potential benefits on offer. Political calculation, ultimately, will determine political reactions.

To fully understand the nature of the European Union, therefore, it is important to reflect on the nature of politics in the member states.

★

While European integration may represent a rational response to the various pressures on national governments, little if any political debate is conducted in such terms. If the EU really does represent a solution to the constrained ability of national governments to act effectively alone – and one wholly consistent with the techniques used to ensure effective policy making within states – why are political leaders so reluctant to say as much?

To answer this question, we need to consider how political leaders have dealt with being increasingly constrained in terms of what they can achieve. While the ability of national governments to deliver what is expected of them has become ever more dependent upon forces outside their direct control, politicians have proved unable and unwilling honestly to acknowledge the fact. This should hardly come as a surprise. The major concern of those in politics is with securing national electoral success. They do so by offering policy choices to electorates. Emphasizing the limits of the possible is hardly an effective strategy to adopt under such circumstances. The aspirant French President Lionel Jospin found this to his cost before the 2002 French Presidential elections, when he was widely criticized for stating that 'I don't think one can administer the economy any more. It is not via laws or texts that we can regulate economics... The whole world is accepting the market.'[8] Why vote for someone, so the argument went, who admits that he can't deliver?

Consequently, there are good grounds for politicians to continue to insist that they alone can solve the problems confronting their populations. Jospin himself was later to declare that:

> We seek to create a regulatory system for the world
> capitalist economy... so that we can influence the
> process of globalization and control its pace for the
> benefit of society... This need to take control in
> adapting to reality places a special responsibility on the
> state... Often it is the only agent that can clear away or
> navigate around the archaic forces standing in the way
> of what society wants.
>
> (*Guardian*, 16 November 1999)

A determination to insist upon the ability of national governments to respond to the myriad pressures upon them leaves little space for an appreciation of the role of the European Union in reinforcing their ability to do so. Indeed, such an appreciation would represent precisely the kind of admission of weakness that politicians shy away from.

Not only is the state portrayed as fully capable of dealing with the challenges confronting it, but politicians have a tendency to discuss a particular form of state. We live, as we have seen, in liberal democratic societies within which the power of popular majorities is constrained by non-majoritarian institutions. Yet politicians have always been more interested in emphasizing the democratic rather than the liberal element of modern government, more interested in fostering the belief that democracy is the power of

the people (and thus of their democratically elected representatives), than in explaining the myriad checks and
balances in place to protect against the tyranny of the
majority. Indeed, they have proven increasingly willing to
challenge these checks and balances. Witness the concerns
of British judges about legislative measures on issues
ranging from sentencing, to control orders for terrorists, to
the judicial review of asylum and immigration decisions –
all of which had the potential to reduce the independent
role of the judiciary.[9]

Talking up the capacities and democratic credentials of
the nation state serves to reinforce the notion that national
governments alone are the rightful decision makers in political life. The purpose and legitimacy of international
institutions are thereby almost inevitably, if implicitly, called
into question. It should come as no surprise, then, if the
Union is often portrayed merely as a non-democratic con-
straint upon the ability of states to do what they want.
Political leaders are not in the habit of admitting they need
help from anyone.

That they act in this way is hardly surprising. They face
overwhelming incentives to allow domestic considerations
to dictate their attitude towards international institutions.
After all, the ultimate rewards of politics are to be found
not in Brussels but in national capitals. Moreover, there is
no real downside to playing the national card in one's dealings with Europe. In no member state is the EU a
particularly salient political issue. Nowhere do politicians
stand to gain from running on a platform of having helped

build a more stable or effective Union. As the Polish President Lech Kaczyński put it (and Polish politicians, when not saying things no one still believes, can generally be counted on to say those things people believe but do not say), 'What interests the Poles is the future of Poland, and not that of the EU.'

The Union stubbornly remains at best a second-order political issue in national capitals, meaning that national debates take precedence, with EU matters generally being seen through their prism. Nowhere is this more clear than in elections to the European Parliament, characterized by fierce debates about national political issues (occasionally including the policies of governments towards the EU). The implications of this are considered in more detail later.

Thus it makes sense for politicians to enhance their domestic popularity even if this comes at the expense of the EU. On those occasions when the Union – fleetingly – becomes a focus for political attention, they tend to emphasize the zero-sum nature of negotiations with 'Brussels' and with other capitals, rather than the collaborative nature of an undertaking designed to compensate for the relative incapacity of individual member states. Tales of battles between competing visions of Europe, whether it be John Major's 'game, set and match' after Maastricht (a good line, albeit not one he actually used), or Mitterrand's description of that same treaty as a 'French project', abound. And they are lapped up by a media far more interested in 'us versus them' struggles for supremacy than in complex explanations of complex interdependencies and the complex institutions created to allow member states to handle them.

Even when political leaders genuinely wish to explain the benefits of integration, political factors may impede their ability to do so. One could be forgiven for having lost count of the number of times that Tony Blair promised to take on 'anti-EU prejudice' in the UK. The incentives he faced as a national politician in a country at best half-hearted in its support for the EU explain both the need for such a campaign and its failure to materialize.

And when the Union does provide obvious benefits, the same incentives ensure that political leaders do not go out of their way to spell these out. The former British Chancellor Gordon Brown was all too willing to hand out lessons on economic management to his European counterparts, yet never seemed to get round to mentioning the role played by the single market in fostering British economic success. This is a phenomenon well known in all multi-levelled political systems, with students of American politics having coined terms such as 'credit assignment problem' to describe the difficulties public authorities face in gaining credit for those things they do well.

Naturally enough, this tendency is all the more marked in those cases where the Union forces upon member states policies – however sensible – that contradict those of the incumbent government. Two British examples are illustrative. In the late 1980s, Margaret Thatcher was desperate to sell Rover. Her government entered into exclusive negotiations with British Aerospace, offering significant cash inducements to get the ailing car manufacturer off its hands. Following the sale, two European Commission investigations led to demands for the repayment by BAe to the British Exchequer of some £331 million in government payments deemed illegal under the EC Treaty. Having repaid the money, the aerospace firm promptly went ahead and purchased Rover anyway. Curiously, the government failed to trumpet the significant savings the Commission had made on behalf of the British taxpayer. Similarly, in 1995, Cyril Richardson won a landmark victory against the British government in front of the EU's court, the European Court of Justice. As a consequence, rules stipulating that men could receive free prescriptions only from the age of sixty-five (the corresponding age for women was sixty) were found to be illegal. Once again, government spokesmen were not seen falling over themselves to proclaim to the public that the Commission had forced them to make prescriptions for the elderly more affordable.

Apart from failing to give credit where credit is due, politicians also benefit from an ability to dump their problems on the Union. There are real benefits to be had for one level of government in entrusting inherently unpopular decisions to another. In the United States, the Supreme Court has been moved to consider the issue, with Justice Scalia enunciating the incentives that might lead the federal government to make states responsible for financing or implementing federal spending programmes:

By forcing state governments to absorb the financial
burden of implementing a federal regulatory program,
Members of Congress can take credit for 'solving'
problems without having to ask their constituents to
pay for the solutions with higher federal taxes. And
even when the States are not forced to absorb the costs
of implementing a federal program, they are still put in
the position of taking the blame for its burdensomeness
and for its defects.

(*Printz* v. *United States*, 1997)

In Europe, the same logic applies in reverse. A member
state can act towards the Union as the US federal government does towards the states. If Brussels can be entrusted
with the task of formulating or implementing policies with
which member state governments would rather not be associated, so much the better. There is always the prospect of
blaming it for subsequent failures. Thus one hears in
Brussels of successive French Finance Ministers, constrained at home by the strength of public sector unions,
begging the European Commission to forbid payments of
public money to nationalized industries, then reaping the
populist spoils by attacking 'Brussels' for acting precisely as
they had requested.

In this sense, entrusting policy-making responsibilities to
international institutions creates a no-lose situation for
politicians. Their popularity will rise when such institutions
make the right decisions, but the latter can equally easily
be blamed for policy failures. National governments can

therefore have their cakes and eat them, blaming the EU for unpopular policies, and failing to credit it for popular ones. The problems come, of course, when those same politicians act in this way and then expect the Union to be popular enough to win public support in referenda about its future.

A further, more subtle explanation for the obfuscation with which national politicians shroud the Union concerns the changing nature of international politics. Some two hundred years ago, Edmund Burke commented scathingly (if prematurely) in his *Reflections on the French Revolution* that the 'age of chivalry is gone. That of sophisters, economists, and calculators has succeeded; and the glory of Europe is extinguished forever.' What was not true then is increasingly so now. Foreign policy used to be sexy. Now, however, because of interdependence and public concern with economic provision, more and more diplomacy concerns issues such as technical trade agreements, regulatory standards and the like. The foreign policy agenda, in other words, is increasingly full of the stuff of domestic politics, and, consequently, less dominated by the traditional, 'heroic' issues of war, peace and diplomacy.

The increasingly dry and technical nature of international politics confronts politicians with a dilemma, particularly in an age when the popular appetite for complex issues seems as limited as it has ever been. It is precisely in their external dealings that they have traditionally aspired to act, or at least appear, as global statesmen, bestriding the world stage. This is a harder trick to pull off when the international politics in question consist of negotiations over the price of butter (whether the Union should be discussing butter prices at all is discussed in chapter 5).

Consequently, there is a tendency to resort to hyperbole, replacing traditional foreign policy language with a new 'transcendental discourse' intended to dramatize the mundane, to create the 'illusion in the minds of the population that governments have been engaged in significant and novel activities'.[10] National dealings with the EU are a case in point. As chapter 2 illustrates, the tendency to dress European integration in the language of a higher purpose dates from its origins. Talk of forging a 'European identity' or of creating a 'United State of Europe' are examples of such rhetoric. They are designed to inspire rather than to explain, to obfuscate rather than clarify, all the while imbuing integration with a misplaced sense of adventure that reflects the insecurity of national political leaders more than it does the nature or purpose of the Union itself.

★

The paradox of integration, therefore, is explicable largely in terms of the paradoxes of national politics. States need international institutions, yet their political leaders are at best slow openly to accept this fact.

The European Union represents a response to an international environment in which states are confronted with strong incentives to collaborate (albeit, as the next chapter shows, that these vary from state to state). Its structure is partly a reflection of the need to ensure effective cooperation; partly, too, a recognition of the fact that the largely economic policies with which it deals are often best handled by independent institutions.

Of course, it was never as simple as this. Politics is not the art of responding rationally to functional requirements. Many rational decisions are never taken, and many irrational ones are. And the existence of the European Union, whatever the abstract justifications that can be provided for its nature, was not and is not an inevitable outcome of the conditions described above.

Rather, as the following chapter shows in more detail, European integration came about as a result of specific and highly contingent historical circumstances. Each such set of circumstances provided new justifications for what was being done, and served merely to add to the increasing confusion, now arguably at its peak, as to the true purpose of the European Union and European Community which preceded it.

2

FROM PEACE TO PROSPERITY

I venture to suggest,' declared Lord Dilhorne to the House of Lords in 1962, 'that the vast majority of men and women in this country will never directly feel the impact of the Community-made law at all.' Forty years later, the assembled leaders of the fifteen member states announced their concern about 'European institutions inveigling their way into every nook and cranny of life'.

The two statements underline the extraordinary expansion in the tasks undertaken by the EC/EU. Since the creation of the European Coal and Steel Community in the early 1950s, the nature and purpose of European integration have changed profoundly. From a community constructed to enable the pooling of coal and steel resources, Europeans have gone on to create a Union with some purview over virtually every aspect of policy.

Two features of this development are particularly worthy of note. First, the history of the EC and EU reveals a consistent core to their activities, albeit one often overlooked in the ambitious political rhetoric that has accompanied their development. From a project designed to promote peace, integration has been transformed into the most ambitious attempt at interstate market creation ever undertaken. Yet, equally striking, the member states, confronted with the implications of the end of the Cold War and collapse of the Berlin Wall, increasingly turned to the European Union (as it became with the ratification of the Maastricht Treaty in 1993) to solve a variety of broader problems, ranging from immigration to monetary instability to security. The Union of today covers significantly more areas of policy than even the EC of the 1980s.

For all this expansion in the EU's tasks, however, this chapter and those that follow it argue that the core of European integration remains the market. Certainly, in the immediate aftermath of the Second World War, market making was inspired by a need to ensure reconciliation between the previously warring states of Western Europe. Yet the Union has developed from an economic project with political objectives into an economic project whose political importance resides largely in its economic significance. The 'high politics' of security have given way to the 'normal politics' of socio-economic contestation; peace has been replaced as the objective by prosperity.[1]

★

The birth of European integration must rank among the most remarkable episodes in European history.[2] West European governments were, in 1945, hardly anxious to engage in collaborative ventures, least of all collaborative ventures involving Germany. The horrors perpetrated by the Nazi regime were seared into the consciousness of European peoples, particularly those of Germany's immediate neighbours. The first halting step towards cooperative European arrangements – the Brussels Treaty of 17 March 1948 – was intended as a guarantee against future German aggression. Yet within five years of the cessation of hostilities, the French Foreign Minister, Robert Schuman, declared to an astonished world that France was willing to pool its coal and steel resources with Germany in an attempt to render war between them impossible.

How was it that this came about? For many at the time, and indeed subsequently, those statesmen responsible for the birth of integration were far-sighted visionaries, quick to understand the limitations of the nation state and anxious to create forms of political organization to replace it and hence prevent a return to European conflict. Yet behind the proliferation of grandiloquent rhetoric about peace, reconciliation and Europe's federal future, narrow national interests and traditional power politics predominated in shaping Europe's institutional landscape.

As intimated in chapter 1, states need strong incentives to engage in institutionalized cooperation. Europe in the 1940s provided just such incentives. And France was the key player. Immediately after the war, French political leaders had two overriding and interlinked objectives. First, to ensure that there could be no revival of the threat from Germany that had seen it invaded three times in seventy years. Second, to lay the foundations for French economic and political revival. The preferred option was to accomplish both simultaneously. François Mauriac neatly summarized French thinking: 'I love Germany so much, I am happy there are two of them.' France would insist on the creation of a divided and economically weakened German state. This could be plundered for those resources – principally coal – necessary to initiate and sustain a French recovery.

Yet the problem for Paris was that its obsession with Germany proved increasingly at odds with the attitudes of its allies. Britain and the United States were coming to perceive the Soviet Union, and not a resurgent Germany, as the single greatest threat to their security. Seen in this light, an enfeebled Germany was a recipe for Communist subversion, if not Red Army invasion. Consequently, and in the face of vociferous French opposition, London and Washington began progressively to lift the economic restrictions imposed on the nascent German state and, in 1947, merged their occupation zones and raised German industrial production levels.

So French political leaders found themselves in a quandary. Their partners were intent on the creation of a German state. And the valuable coal resources of the Ruhr lay within the British zone of occupation. They could thus either object, and alienate the new German state from birth, or find an alternative means of gaining access to the coal reserves upon which France's fragile economic recovery depended.

Left without a viable alternative, France agreed, via the London accords of June 1948, to the creation of what was to become the Federal Republic of Germany. British and American insistence that a punitive German policy was unworkable in the context of the nascent Cold War led Paris to accept the previously unthinkable, though not without insisting that the new German state be a decentralized, federal entity.[3]

And once the Federal Republic had come into being, Paris had little choice but to cooperate with it. Put in terms of Rousseau's stag hunt, collaboration held out the prospect of venison for the foreseeable future via negotiated access to German resources. Hostility, in contrast, would have provided an anorexic hare. The genesis of European integration, therefore, lay not in memories of the past war but, rather, in anticipation of the next. A potent combination of practical necessity and profound insecurity led France, along with the Benelux states, to conceive the inconceivable and contemplate cooperation with the post-war West German state.

The specific solution arrived at was the joint management of coal and steel resources via the creation of independent institutions to manage policy in these sectors. Not even overwhelming necessity could prevent bitter wrangles between the participants over the details of the scheme. Thus, special provisions were provided for Italian steel (notably being allowed to maintain tariffs for five years) and Belgian coal, while angry squabbles characterized discussions of the location of the new institutions.[4] Yet eventually, the first institutions of European integration came into being (albeit shared – in what proved to be a dangerous precedent – between Brussels, Strasbourg and Luxembourg), in the shape of the European Coal and Steel Community (ECSC).

Such skirmishes should not obscure the revolutionary nature of what was actually achieved. The French were forced into coming up with a novel solution to their resource dependence problem. Their preferred option had been to take what they wanted from Germany unilaterally. Virulent fear and distrust of Germany pervaded their country. Thus to have come up with such a creative solution required political imagination and courage of the first order.

Moreover, while the idea of pooling coal and steel resources might not set the contemporary pulse racing, its significance at the time can hardly be overstated. By agreeing to the creation of regional institutions, Europe's most persistent foes were putting behind them decades of conflict that had centred around the rich coal fields of eastern France and western Germany. They were agreeing, in effect, to share their war-making potential. As Robert Schuman put it in his declaration of 9 May 1950, the 'solidarity in production thus established will make it plain that any war between France and Germany becomes not merely unthinkable, but materially impossible'.

The birth of the ECSC established three crucial precedents. First, that European initiatives should be accompanied by lofty rhetoric. The coal and steel community hardly lacked resonance in its own right. Yet this was not enough.

Institutional creation, as so often in the years that followed, was to be legitimized in terms of a transcendental theme. Thus, Schuman declared, the Community would 'lay the first concrete foundation for a European Federation'.

Second, the Coal and Steel Community provided the institutional model that would, in slightly amended form, characterize both the European Community and the European Union that succeeded it. The ECSC introduced the principle of juxtaposing a Council as a traditional forum for interstate negotiation between national representatives, alongside an institution intended to act in the 'European' interest – the High Authority, precursor of the European Commission.

Finally, the institutional trappings of the Coal and Steel Community betrayed the longer-term ambitions of its creators. Its highly complex institutional structure – which included a Court and an Assembly – was out of kilter with its limited role in managing coal and steel. The disjuncture between form and function was a measure of the desire of some, reflected in Schuman's rhetoric about steps towards federation, to see a community initially intended to manage coal and steel develop into a more far-reaching regional organization.

No sooner had Schuman made his declaration than events intervened. The catalyst was the North Korean invasion of its southern neighbour. In the fevered atmosphere of the time, many viewed events in East Asia merely as a precursor to the arrival of the Red Army in Western Europe. Konrad Adenauer declared himself 'convinced that Stalin has the same plan for Europe as for Korea. What is happening there is a dress-rehearsal for what is in store for us here.'[5]

The Korean War led to American insistence that the West needed German troops in order to defend itself against the Red threat. This was hardly an idea calculated to inspire enthusiasm on the part of Germany's neighbours. And so, confronted once again with American pressure, the French resorted to the approach they had dreamt up to secure access to coal. In October 1950, they proposed the creation of a European Defence Community (EDC) within which West German troops could be safely merged into a greater European whole, thus avoiding the need for a new Wehrmacht.

The scope and significance of this are hard to exaggerate. The ECSC Assembly was directed to draft a constitution for a political body to provide direction to the new European army. What was being proposed was, in all but name, a European federation. As it turned out, the EDC collapsed following a vote in France (on this occasion in the National Assembly in 1954). If the sight of triumphant communist deputies singing the 'Marseillaise' in unison with colleagues from the political right was incongruous, it too presaged later debates about integration.

With defence and security removed from the agenda of European integration (Germany simply joined NATO), the six signatories of the ECSC Treaty turned to a plan by the Dutch Foreign Minister, Jan Willem Beyen, for the creation of an industrial customs union. The Beyen Plan was discussed by Foreign Ministers at Messina in June 1955,

leading to detailed negotiations for the creation of a
European Economic Community. Once again, negotiations
were complex and occasionally vitriolic. The problems
inherent in attempting to integrate a number of mixed
economies were immediately in evidence as agreement
proved impossible – and this at the height of Keynesian economic orthodoxy – on an industrial or regional policy for
the new community. Indeed, that agreement was reached at
all was largely due to the willingness of the Federal
Republic to make concessions to France over the inclusion
of an agricultural policy, the creation of a Community for
nuclear energy – EURATOM – and the inclusion in the
common market of French overseas territories.

Immediately apparent from even a cursory reading of the
text of the Treaty of Rome is that, less than a decade after
the Schuman declaration, the nature of European integration had changed fundamentally. The EEC was still
provided with a Court and an Assembly alongside the
Council and Commission. But the federalist window of
opportunity that may have been ajar during the EDC negotiations was now firmly (and thankfully) closed. In contrast
to the Treaty of Paris, that of Rome entrusted significantly
less authority to the European Commission than had been
provided for the High Authority. The fact that the EEC
covered the whole economy made the risks of creating powerful independent institutions too great for the member
states to contemplate. Typically, however, the Treaty of
Rome – ratified by the six and signed on 25 March 1957 –
declares confidently in its preamble that the EC was a means

to 'an ever closer union among the peoples of Europe'.

European integration was thus the consequence of a number of highly contingent historical processes. It was only because of the Second World War that the nation states of Western Europe found themselves so enfeebled as to seek cooperation. It was only because of the Cold War that France could be persuaded to adopt a cooperative approach to Germany. And even in the relatively short period between the Schuman declaration and the Treaty of Rome, the nature of integration altered profoundly. By 1958, early federalist ambitions, so obvious in the Treaty of Paris and in Schuman's declaration which had foreshadowed it, were watered down. In the wake of the failure of the openly federalist EDC, member states reasserted themselves and focused their collaborative efforts on the economy.

★

During the thirty or so years following the signing of the Treaty of Rome, this shift to economic management was entrenched. Not that European leaders lost their penchant for high-profile political 'projects'. The period witnessed a series of such schemes, ranging from Charles de Gaulle's repeated initiatives aimed at creating a Europe capable of rivalling the United States on the world stage, to attempts to formulate a common approach to energy policy in response to the 1973 oil shock. Yet all such schemes foundered, underlining the limitations of integration in high-profile, politically sensitive sectors.

Indeed, de Gaulle himself underlined continued sensitivities about national autonomy in contriving to initiate what
remains the worst crisis in the history of integration. In
1965, he brought the EEC to a standstill when, in protest at
Commission plans to introduce a new budgetary system and
increase the powers of the European Parliamentary
Assembly, he withdrew French representatives from the
Council of Ministers. The row presaged long years of unease
about the dangers of 'supranationalism', or decisions taken
by institutions not formally controlled by the member
states themselves.[6]

In the academic literature, interest in the EC waned, as
developments in the 1970s failed to reflect the hopes and
predictions (the two are generally linked) of either its
founders or those American social scientists who had dominated its study. Federalist dreams evaporated. Rather than
the eagerly anticipated steady increase in the authority and
assertiveness of the European Commission, and concomitant decline in the role of the member states, national
capitals came to play an increasingly prominent role in the
EC. By the latter half of the 1970s, the French President,
Giscard d'Estaing, during his *tours de table* at meetings of
European Heads of State and Government, had taken to
ignoring the Commission President completely. Indeed, the
unfamiliar names of the first Commission Presidents of the
1970s – Jean Rey, Franco Maria Malfatti, Sicco Mansholt
and François-Xavier Ortoli – are illustrative of the declining
relevance of the institution.

The sense of disappointment was merely exacerbated by

the ambitious rhetoric which accompanied these developments. The assembled signatories chose the declaration that
emerged from the 1969 Hague summit to emphasize their
'belief in the political objectives which gave the Community
its meaning and purport', while committing themselves to
the achievement of Economic and Monetary Union (EMU).
The following year, the Werner Plan of October 1970 called
for the achievement of Economic and Monetary Union
within ten years. Two years later, the October 1972 Paris
summit solemnly declared that the 'member states of the
Community, the driving force of European construction,
affirm their intention before the end of the present decade
to transform the whole complex of their relations into a
European Union'.

The lattermost statement was revelatory in at least two
respects. First, it underlined again the propensity of
member states to resort to the transcendental when in need
of inspiration (or needing to inspire). The notion of
'European Union' has, to this day, not been adequately
defined, but it sounds ambitious, and serves to raise hopes
(or fears). Second, whatever it may in fact be, 'political
union' is not necessarily compatible with member states
remaining the 'driving force of European construction'.
Given the experience of de Gaulle's 1965 protest, it was
clear even in 1972 that increasing the scope of a community
run by interstate unanimity could prove a recipe simply for
immobilism. Dissimulation, contradiction and obfuscation.
The pattern was set.

All this at the very moment when such grandiose ambi-

tions were least achievable. From the early 1970s, enlargement began fundamentally to alter the nature of
integration. In 1973, Denmark, Ireland and the UK acceded
to the EC. In 1978 and 1979, negotiations started with
Portugal and Spain respectively. Greek accession followed
in 1981. Enlargement brought into the fold states relatively
inured to the historical association between peace and integration. If the creation of the ECSC represented the
launching of an economic project for explicitly political
ends, the entrants of 1973 viewed integration as an economic project aimed at achieving economic objectives. For
the Greeks, as for the Spanish and Portuguese after them, a
political element existed – but this was the association
between accession and the preservation of their own democratic systems, rather than the notion of the EC as a
promoter of interstate peace. Henceforth, member state
agreement on the purpose of integration could not be
assumed.

Yet, for all this, the 1970s were not as fallow as some
have claimed. The real achievements, however, occurred
away from the public gaze and the razzamatazz of the
regular meetings of European Heads of State and
Government that had begun to occur. Although little
remarked upon, the European market foreseen in the Treaty
of Rome represented perhaps the most significant achievement. Market creation proceeded apace aided, no doubt, by
the propitious prevailing economic conditions of high
growth and low unemployment and inflation.[7] The first
intra-EU tariff reductions took place on 1 January 1959. By

1968, the customs union was completed – eighteen months ahead of schedule. The erection of a Common External Tariff meant that the European Commission represented the Community in both the Dillon and Kennedy rounds of General Agreement on Tariffs and Trade (GATT) talks. JFK was moved to comment, as early as January 1962, that an 'economy which may soon nearly equal our own, protected by a single external tariff similar to our own, has progressed with such success and momentum that it has surpassed its original timetable, convinced those initially sceptical that there is now no turning back...'

Sceptics are, I fear, even now not so convinced, but Kennedy's endorsement was striking nonetheless. And progress in market creation was buttressed by startling developments in the legal sphere. These encapsulated perfectly the disjuncture, central to any appreciation of European integration, between the profile of events and their significance. Few people know, or want to know, about ureaformaldehyde. Still fewer (I would guess) care about the regulations governing imports of it into the Netherlands in the 1960s. Yet this issue was to spark little short of a legal revolution.

'Normal' international treaties are binding upon their constituent states and not the individuals within them. Yet when, in 1962, a Dutch importer of ureaformaldehyde alleged in a Dutch national court that new tariff arrangements for the chemical were illegal under the EC Treaty, the European Court of Justice delivered a path-breaking judgment in response to the resultant query from the Dutch legal authorities. Indicative of the perceived importance of the case was the fact that three of the six member states intervened to argue that Community law could not apply directly to individuals. Yet the Court disagreed:

> This Treaty is more than an agreement which merely
> creates mutual obligations between the contracting
> states... The Community constitutes a new legal order
> in international law, for whose benefit the states have
> limited their sovereign rights... and the subjects of
> which comprise not only the Member States but also
> their nationals. Community law therefore... not only
> imposes obligations on individuals but also confers on
> them legal rights.

The Dutch importer therefore had a legal right to expect its government to respect the EC Treaty. The bottom line was that the law of the Community was effectively transformed into something more akin to the law *within* than that *between* states. Individuals were empowered to use it to challenge the actions of their own governments, a right that has subsequently represented a crucial means of ensuring the effective application of EC law (as explained in chapter 3).

Less than twelve months later, the impact of the *Van Gend* judgment was reinforced. Once again, the technical details are of little relevance. What is important is that, in response to a reference for clarification from an Italian court, the European Court of Justice ruled that, when it came into conflict with national law, Community law would take precedence.

Both judgments made perfect logical sense. In their absence, member states could either fail to apply EU law, regardless of the consequences for individuals or private firms, or pass new laws contradicting whatever was agreed at the EU level. Either option would make a mockery of the notions of community law and a common European market. And the market implications of the Community's legal system were made fully apparent slightly over a decade later, when the Court ruled on a dispute between Germany and the French manufacturers of the liqueur Cassis de Dijon, whose sale was prohibited by the German authorities.

The Court stated that there was 'no valid reason why, provided they have been lawfully produced and marketed in one of the Member States, alcoholic beverages should not be introduced into any other Member State'. Technical German regulations specifying appropriate alcohol content for certain kinds of drinks could not, in other words, be invoked to prevent the import of Cassis and protect the German market. National governments could be overruled when it came to regulating their own markets if these regulations came into conflict with European law.

The implications of the case, moreover, went far wider than the ability of German consumers to purchase the key ingredient of what is a highly alcoholic form of Ribena. What the Court had done, in effect, was come up with an ingenious solution to a problem that had been plaguing attempts to create a European market. The Commission had hitherto assumed that the only way to do this was via a process of 'harmonization'. This implied that different regulations in the member states would be replaced by a single, EC regulation. Yet the requirement for unanimity in the Council meant that agreement on such regulations often proved elusive. The principle of 'mutual recognition', whereby goods legally manufactured in one state could be sold legally in the others – unless there was a good reason why this should not be the case – was to prove a powerful weapon in the battle to create a single market.

Still other initiatives were designed to supplement and strengthen the market. With British accession looming, member states reached agreement on the EC budget, with the Community gaining its 'own resources' drawn from customs duties, agricultural levies and a percentage of VAT revenue. Related to discussions over the budget was the decision to create a regional development fund, in part as a pay-off for the potential costs of enlargement. For the first time, therefore, the EC took some responsibility for regional disparities within and between its member states. Finally, currency fluctuations between the member states were increasingly perceived as damaging, given the expanding volume of intra-EC trade. In December 1979, agreement was reached on the creation of an Exchange Rate Mechanism (ERM), limiting fluctuations between the currencies of the participating states to a defined margin (while the ERM was not formally part of the Community, membership was open only to those member states that chose to participate).

The two decades following the signing of the Rome Treaty, therefore, saw much progress made in the creation of the market and its legal underpinnings. And this was all the more striking given the prevailing economic conditions, particularly following the oil shocks of 1973 and the onset of stagflation – the word coined for the new and insidious combination of low growth and spiralling inflation. That member states used integration at all during a period of such economic turbulence, when it would have been equally easy for them to turn inwards and ignore the Community completely, was striking testament to its continued relevance.

★

While hindsight allows us to be relatively positive about the achievements of the 1970s, this was not the case in the early 1980s. As we've seen, on the occasion of the twenty-fifth anniversary of the signing of the Treaty of Rome, *The Economist* published on its cover a tombstone proclaiming the death of the EC. Enlargement negotiations with Spain and Portugal had stalled over the difficult issues of textiles and agriculture (France was concerned about the potential for cheap imports from these countries undermining its own industries). Following re-election in 1983, Margaret Thatcher was increasingly bullish about the need for a permanent resolution to the British budgetary issue. This had been a bone of contention since British accession in 1973. Hardly surprisingly, since Paris had made agreement on a

new budgetary package guaranteeing agricultural funding
(and hence affecting Britain particularly negatively, as
London stood to gain little from such funding) a condition
of agreeing to UK membership in the first place. Indicative
of the sour atmosphere, the December 1983 Athens meeting of Heads of State and Government, uniquely, failed to
agree on a final communiqué.

Moreover, for all the tariff reductions, for all the progress
in monetary cooperation, for all the rulings of the Court,
the European economies were simply not working. The economic situation had worsened again after the second oil
shock of 1979, which sparked a huge rise in unemployment. The major success of the Community had lain in the
removal of tariff barriers and quantitative restrictions on
trade between member states. Yet, faced with spiralling
inflation and unemployment, member states found other
ways to protect their economies from foreign competition.
Non-tariff barriers proliferated, ranging from governmental funding (state aid) to support the development of
'national champions', to a myriad technical and administrative regulations (such as those that had blocked the import
of Cassis), whose effect was to close the national market to
foreign goods. The EC in the early 1980s still resembled a
patchwork of national rules and regulations, many of which
were designed to hinder the access of foreign goods, services and workers.

That this situation had been allowed to arise was partly a
function of the emphasis on harmonization referred to
above. Partly, too, it stemmed from the timidity of the

European Commission in carrying out its task of ensuring respect for the treaty. The Court may have declared the supremacy of EC law, but if the Commission failed to ensure its implementation, it mattered not a jot. This was underlined by the British Prime Minister, James Callaghan. In an attempt to reassure the General Secretary of the Labour Party about the impact of EC membership, he listed four examples of state aid provided by the British government to industry, all, he proudly pointed out, illegal under the EC Treaty, yet all overlooked by a European Commission anxious to avoid confrontation.[8]

Yet the key problem, and, as it turned out, the basis for a resolution, lay in the member states. It required political consensus for the Community to focus its attention on market creation. The fact that the member states, who had so assiduously erected rules to protect their markets during the 1970s, were eventually able to strike agreement on the need for their removal in the following decade was due to several factors. The first was their ability to sort out the other issues cluttering the EC agenda. The British budgetary dispute was finally brought to an end at the Fontainebleau summit of March 1984, with the introduction of a permanent compensation mechanism (the infamous 'rebate') to take account of the disproportionate net contribution of the UK. The following year, an answer was found to Greek demands for financial assistance in dealing with the costs of adjustment to membership and the anticipated costs of the forthcoming enlargement to Spain and Portugal (the Integrated Mediterranean Programme was created in

1985). Not for the first, and certainly not for the last time, side-payments proved necessary to entice member states into further integrative steps.

Second, whatever their ideological proclivities, all member state governments had come to feel increasingly frustrated at Europe's poor economic performance. The growing economic, and particularly technological, gap between Europe on the one hand and Japan and the United States on the other was, by the early 1980s, a source of serious concern not only for politicians but also for multi-national European businesses. These latter began to lobby hard for a European solution to the situation, as the idea began to take root that the EC's relatively weak performance was partly attributable to the fragmentation of its market.

Agreement on the shape of a strategy to address these shortcomings was facilitated by broad convergence between a new generation of political leaders. It is important not to overstate this: Margaret Thatcher, Helmut Kohl and François Mitterrand were hardly ideological soulmates. And as we shall see in chapter 4, many of the problems currently bedevilling attempts to complete the market can be traced back to the ambiguity of the deal that they eventually managed to strike. Yet such ambiguity, and a willingness to put off difficult decisions – particularly concerning the degree to which the European market should be regulated – was a *sine qua non* for agreement on the need for a market at all. In the event, a broad consensus began to emerge around the need for a supply-side focus and market creation among politicians ranging from Thatcher, with her desire to create a liberal European market, to Mitterrand and his aspirations for a *Europe sociale*.

Finally, the European Commission, under its new French President, Jacques Delors, proved a subtle and effective operator. From the early 1980s, the institution had lobbied in favour of the completion of the single market. As member state sentiment coalesced around the idea, it skilfully constructed a coalition. Delors was adept at adjusting his language to suit his audience: the emphasis on social Europe that earned him a standing ovation at the 1988 Labour Party conference was far different to the stress on deregulation that helped woo Margaret Thatcher.[9] As importantly, the Commission White Paper, drafted by Delors and the British Commissioner Lord Cockfield, and approved by the European Council at Milan in June 1985, was dry and technical. Not for nothing was Lord Cockfield once referred to as the only man who spoke like a White Paper. His own such paper listed almost three hundred technical measures required to complete the market, while remaining silent on any implications the ambitious programme might have either financially or in terms of national sovereignty.[10]

Yet implications there were aplenty. For one thing, the Single European Act – the wholesale treaty revision carried out to implement the market programme (signed in February 1986 and in force in July 1987) – made provision for an extension of qualified majority voting (QMV) in the Council, in an attempt to overcome the legislative logjams created by the unanimity requirement. Inevitably, the scope of QMV was limited, with consensus remaining necessary in the areas of fiscal policy, the free movement of persons and employee rights, yet the decision to extend it was significant nonetheless.

For another, agreement on the market required a series of compromises and trade-offs that involved extending the scope of the Community into several new spheres. Thus, in an effort to assuage the concerns of those worried about excessive economic liberalism, the treaty also included provisions on social policy, and in particular for QMV on 'health and safety of workers'. This was to prove highly contentious in the years to come (see chapter 4).

The other trade-off was between the richer and poorer member states. The latter group, bolstered by the accession, in 1986, of Spain and Portugal, feared that the market would disproportionately benefit their richer counterparts and argued long and hard for cash side-payments as compensation.[11] This they received in the form of 'cohesion policy'. Following the signature of the treaty, the 'Club Med' countries (Spain, Portugal and Greece) plus Ireland began to push for a still more generous funding mechanism. Owing largely to the willingness of the German Chancellor, Helmut Kohl, to underwrite the deal, the so-called Delors package was signed in February 1988. It provided for an increase in EC expenditure in the period 1988–92 (to around 1.2 per cent of EC gross national income), incorporating a doubling of regional (known as structural) funds as a compensation to the poorer member states for the anticipated financial consequences of the single market.

The Single Act marked a watershed in the history of European integration. Not only did the member states rally round the new 'project' of creating a true single market by the (non-binding) deadline of 1992. Their enthusiasm, and the zeal with which the Commission set about selling it, had significant practical implications – even beyond the fact that the (Italian) winning entry in the 1990 Eurovision song contest was entitled 'Altogether 1992'. Crucially, the market captured the interest and attention of the business community, as encapsulated by the 'merger mania' that accompanied it. Companies rushed to consolidate their positions within the new Europe-wide economic space. In 1987 there were sixty-eight major mergers and acquisitions in the EC. The following year, 300 occurred.[12]

The member states themselves echoed this enthusiasm. Inspired by the notion of an economic area without internal frontiers, France, Germany and the Benelux states in 1985 signed the Schengen agreement, providing for a border-free zone. Externally, the market prompted fears on the part of non-members that they would miss out on the benefits it promised to provide. Austria applied for membership in 1989 and its European Free Trade Area (EFTA) partners Norway, Sweden and Finland had all done likewise by 1992.

Equally significantly, monetary union appeared back on the EC stage for the first time since its ill-fated cameo in the 1970s. It made little sense, so its proponents argued, to remove barriers to economic exchange if the existence of numerous different currencies itself constituted such a barrier, particularly via the fees charged by banks for currency conversions. The June 1988 Hanover European Council had agreed to the liberalization of all capital movements by December 1992, opening up the prospect of increased speculation against member state currencies. The same meeting therefore authorized Delors to formulate a plan for EMU. A committee was set up (generally a sign of enthusiasm in the Union), chaired by the Commission President and including senior officials from the central banks of the member states. The report it delivered to the Madrid Council of 1989 was approved, as, too, was a decision to call an intergovernmental conference to discuss its implementation and the move to monetary union.

Last, but not least, and as much through happy coincidence as the impact of the still nascent market, the economic performance of the Community improved massively. In the heady early days of the single market programme, it appeared that integration was marching towards a brighter future.

★

Dark clouds, however, lay heavy on the horizon. The very successes of the Community led to increasing concerns about it. Delors in particular began to cause consternation in national capitals with his ambitious rhetoric. In a widely publicized speech before the European Parliament in 1988, he claimed that within ten years, 'eighty per cent of our economic legislation and perhaps even our fiscal and social legislation as well, will be of Community origin'. Hardly words designed to reassure national political leaders or their publics. Nor, for that matter, the last time that a Europhile proved more effective than any Eurosceptic propaganda in inciting distrust of integration.[13] In 1991, Delors compounded his error with a speech at the International Institute of Strategic Studies in London in which he raised the prospect of a security role for the EC. A Commission President setting out an agenda for an area often seen as representing the apotheosis of national competence was reckless to say the least. All the more so as Delors's role in securing agreement on the adoption of a flag and anthem for the EC had already been interpreted by many as indicative of his state-building ambitions. These ambitions found metaphorical expression in the so-called 'bicycle theory' of integration, popular at the time, according to which the survival of the EC, like the balance of a cyclist, depended on constant forward motion.

Rumblings of discontent about the apparent ambitions of 'Brussels' had been audible as early as the late 1980s, most notably in Margaret Thatcher's infamous Bruges speech of 1988, during which she had pronounced that 'We have not successfully rolled back the frontiers of the state in Britain, only to see them reimposed at a European level, with a European superstate exercising a new dominance from Brussels.' Such sentiments merely intensified and became more widespread as the Commission President became more outspoken and as both the Court and the Commission became more assertive in enforcing EC law to open the market. No longer could a British Prime Minister proudly trumpet, as Jim Callaghan had done, the meaningless nature of treaty provisions. Governmental attempts to fund firms were increasingly blocked, while member state implementation of single market legislation was more closely tracked.

In the UK, unease was best symbolized by the 'Up yours Delors' headline gracing the front page of the *Sun* on 1 December 1990. Yet it was not confined to Britain. Numerous member states, including France and Germany, challenged attempted Commission interventions in sensitive areas, including culture, education and public health.[14] And national politicians began to speak openly of the need to 'rein in' increasingly assertive EC institutions that were directly challenging them.

Delors's political naivety was not the only source of national wariness. As the Commission President ratcheted up his rhetoric, so, too, were governments coming to realize the full significance of the single market project to which they had committed themselves.

Many of the crucial developments in European integration had, as we have seen, occurred far from the public and even political gaze. Court judgments concerning supremacy, direct effect or mutual recognition resonated only within the relatively few specialist law journals. Even political leaders in the member states largely failed to react. The fact is that, since its creation in the 1950s, the European Community had, as Lord Dilhorne observed, failed to impinge directly on either national publics or national politics. The single market changed this. As a consequence, the Community began to intrude more directly in ever more sensitive areas of national political and economic life. No longer could political leaders sign up to European integration happy in the knowledge that their electorates would neither know nor care. Henceforth, integration was news, of interest to publics, and therefore politically highly salient. However – and with exquisite irony – as their concerns about integration were reaching a peak, the member states found themselves increasingly tempted to use it more widely.

The end of the Cold War was, of course, a seismic event, though its implications took many years to unfold. Yet, from the need to deal with the newly liberated states of Central and Eastern Europe, to the violence in the former Yugoslavia, to the problems of illegal migration and organized crime it spawned, the various policy problems to which it gave birth eluded strictly national solutions; hence the lure of more collaborative action within an EC framework. The first indication of this was provided as early as July 1989, when member states entrusted to the Commission the task of coordinating Western assistance to the newly liberated states of Central and Eastern Europe. This decision was the first in a long line dumping on the EC policy problems that member states either could not, or did not want to tackle alone. 'Competence dumping' was accompanied, however, with increasing suspicion of the EC institutions, with often damaging consequences.

It was in this context – of growing dissatisfaction with

Community institutions whose necessity was increasing – that the member states met at Maastricht. Both tendencies are apparent in the document that emerged from their deliberations.

On the one hand, the Maastricht Treaty (more properly known as the European Union Treaty) significantly expanded the scope of integration to cover a variety of new policy challenges. The most important substantive development was a commitment to move towards monetary union. The new strategic landscape was a crucial determinant of this. 'History,' wrote Mark Twain, 'doesn't repeat itself. But it does rhyme.' The 'German problem' of the 1990s was eerily reminiscent, both in its nature and in the approach adopted towards it, of the events of the late 1940s. This time, however, the Deutschmark and not the Wehrmacht was the source of concern. Remarkably enough, this did not prevent political leaders from speaking as if nothing had changed in the intervening years. Germany's Chancellor Kohl, perhaps the staunchest advocate of monetary union, repeatedly made statements to the effect that the 'nation state is associated with war, and should be superseded by European integration'.[15]

Even prior to German unification, various members of the Exchange Rate Mechanism were expressing concern about German domination of the system. Unification merely heightened fears of a new, economic, German hegemony in Europe. The abandonment of national currencies represented an unprecedented concession of both practical and symbolic national sovereignty. Yet, as history rhymed away, practical need and profound insecurity coincided as they had for Robert Schuman. The combination of dissatisfaction with existing arrangements and fear of the potential influence of a united Germany proved sufficient. Member states, just as in the 1950s, embarked upon what one observer had characterized as a 'headlong flight into an unknown future in order to escape from a fearful present'.[16]

And, of course, a detailed policy response already existed in the form of the report produced by the Delors Committee. Little wonder, then, that the national representatives negotiating in the context of the Intergovernmental Conference on Economic and Monetary Union – one half of the proceedings at Maastricht – simply took this off the shelf and incorporated its three-stage approach to EMU. The treaty set the latest date for entry into the final stage – the irrevocable fixing of exchange rates – as 1 January 1999.

Just as, in the 1940s, Germany had seen its acceptance back into the family of European nations as its reward for integration, so at Maastricht its leaders saw political integration as the prize to be won in exchange for the sacrifice of the Mark. It was at German insistence that parallel negotiations took place on 'political union'. These led to two main sets of treaty provisions. Those on 'Justice and Home Affairs' introduced cooperation in law enforcement, criminal justice, civil judicial matters, and asylum and immigration. As innovatively, the introduction of a 'Common Foreign and Security Policy' marked a new departure, with the treaty calling for greater cooperation between member states in this sphere, and holding out the prospect of the 'eventual framing of a common defence policy, which might in time lead to a common defence'.

Enter the schizophrenia. While the Maastricht Treaty extended the scope of integration to new sectors, it also reflected growing member state unease about what many perceived as excessively powerful EC institutions. This was most clearly exemplified in the 'subsidiarity clause', intended to restrict the actions of the Union to areas where member states could not achieve their objectives acting alone.[17] The treaty also introduced the so-called pillar structure, with the EC being supplemented by separate pillars for Justice and Home Affairs and the Common Foreign and Security Policy, with the EU as the umbrella over all three. This too was explicitly intended to rein in the supranational institutions and to establish member state control over policy formulation in new – and politically sensitive – areas. Decision making here would be by unanimity, with a minimal role for the European Commission.[18]

The one exception to the rule was the Parliament. The combination of the increasing importance of the single market and the provision for qualified majority voting on many market-related measures made the member states aware of the need for some kind of democratic oversight. Because the EP existed, because, therefore, empowering it was easy, because it had been democratically elected (since 1979) and was therefore a more forceful lobbyist for its own powers, because certain member states still harboured their federalist ambition of seeing the EU turn into something akin to a state, the so-called co-decision procedure was introduced, giving the EP an effective right of veto over legislation.

As at The Hague some twenty years earlier, the tensions inherent in member state attitudes were encapsulated in the notion of European Union. On the one hand, it implied closer relations between states, something above and beyond mere international cooperation. On the other, the Union, with its elaborate pillar structure, was created precisely in order to preserve the freedom of manouevre of these member states. Rhetoric versus reality, ambition versus fears, these are the tensions that have haunted the Union to this day.

Just as had occurred following the Single Act, budgetary trade-offs followed treaty negotiations. The Commission released its proposals for a Delors 2 package mere days after the Maastricht Treaty was signed in February 1992. And, once more, the core element of the final deal was an agreement that there would be a large increase in the funds available to the poorer member states. Ominously, however, the negotiations were characterized by resistance on the part of some to such an increase.

The Maastricht Treaty was eventually ratified. However, initial defeat in a referendum in Denmark in June 1992, along with an uncomfortably close outcome in France, ought to have concerned political leaders far more than they ultimately did. The European project they had been engaged in for decades behind the backs of their populations was starting to impinge upon these latter and to concern them.

Meanwhile, enlargement continued apace. In January

1995, Sweden, Austria and Finland acceded to the Union. The whole thing passed off virtually unnoticed, as one would expect of the accession of small, rich states. The next round of enlargement, however, was a different kettle of fish. The 1993 Copenhagen summit laid down the conditions for entry of the Central and East European states. The Luxembourg European Council of 1997 invited the Czech Republic, Estonia, Hungary, Poland and Slovenia to start accession talks; two years later, a similar invitation was extended to Bulgaria, Latvia, Lithuania, Romania and Slovakia. All in all, including the tiny Mediterranean states of Cyprus and Malta, the forthcoming enlargement would encompass a potential twelve states, many of whom were only just emerging from years of communist rule.

The challenge of enlargement led member states to conclude that there was a need for fundamental institutional reform. Yet, enlargement or not, their increasingly hard-nosed attitudes to treaty negotiations meant that the Amsterdam summit of 1997 failed to deliver. The best they could come up with was an agreement to disagree and to try again. This they duly did, with negotiations culminating in a spectacularly bad-tempered summit in Nice in December 2000. This witnessed France falling out with Britain over defence matters, the small member states protesting furiously at attempts by President Chirac to 'bull-doze' them into accepting a smaller share of votes on EU legislation and all member states failing to agree on changes in the composition of the European Commission. And after all that, very little of substance was agreed upon.

At the same time as they were failing to agree upon institutional reforms, the member states were also struggling to reshape existing EU policies in preparation for enlargement. Negotiations over the Agenda 2000 action programme, intended to fix financial priorities for the period 2000–2006, were difficult and fractious. The final negotiations in Berlin were marked by the emergence of a so-called 'net contributors' club' (Austria, France, Germany, the Netherlands, Sweden and the UK), which opposed further significant increases in the EU budget. Confronting the need to deal with the substantial cost of integrating the eastern side of the country, Germany for the first time cast doubt upon its continued role as the paymaster of European integration. It was only when faced with the prospect of a breakdown in negotiations that Chancellor Schroeder finally agreed to reach for his chequebook, though the attacks to which he was subjected by the German media served notice that the Union would not henceforth be able to count on German munificence.

Yet, as institutional and budgetary discussions stalled, monetary union continued apace, and this despite the currency crisis that culminated on Black Wednesday in September 1992, leading to a broadening to 15 per cent of the ERM's currency fluctuation bands. Governments made real efforts to get their public finances into shape in order to meet the convergence criteria (though several among them ultimately depended on liberal interpretations of these criteria to qualify for membership). In March 1998 the Brussels summit accepted the recommendation from the

European Monetary Institute that eleven member states could join stage three in January 1999. On 1 January 2002, euro notes and coins were introduced.

Market integration also continued apace. In 1997, the Commission launched its single market action plan, identifying key priorities for the years ahead. It followed this up by a decision to publish regular scorecards, publicizing the performance of the individual member states in putting single market legislation into place. Anyone who doubted the complexity and centrality of the single market could do no better than talk to one of the countless Central and East European officials charged with carrying out the accession negotiations. Tens of thousands of pages of the *acquis* – the body of existing EU laws – largely dealing with the single market needed to be transposed to the statute books of the applicant states.

And on top of all this, the member states continued to react to the challenges facing them with a raft of new initiatives. Never mind that they couldn't agree on institutional reform. Never mind that they didn't want to spend more. Never mind that the public was increasingly disenchanted with the Union. The Amsterdam Treaty introduced the idea of the EU as an Area of Freedom, Security and Justice and the first AFSJ action plan was introduced in December 1998. Following a Franco-British summit at Saint-Malo in December 1998, the Union rapidly created its European Security and Defence Policy, involving European integration for the first time in the military sphere. In the economic realm, as the downturn of the early 1990s strengthened popular uncertainty about integration, unemployment shot up and business confidence dipped. In response, the Commission adopted the language of competitiveness, and proposed measures such as the promotion of labour market flexibility and the reduction of non-wage costs. In January 1997, Delors's successor, Jacques Santer, proposed an EU employment pact. And at Lisbon in 2000 the EU summit set down ambitious targets related to growth and employment (see chapter 5).

Member states were mixing a potent cocktail. The more they launched initiatives, the more sensitive were the areas of national life impinged on by the EU. Simultaneously, enlargement implied a reduction of their influence within the Union. As early as March 1994, the 'Ioannina Compromise' had illustrated their increasing wariness, effectively lowering the number of votes needed to constitute a blocking minority in the Council. Rising stakes and rising numbers threatened to undermine the trust between them that had allowed integration to proceed as far as it had.

The failures at Amsterdam and Nice provided further evidence of this trend. As a result, the member states agreed on the need for a broader debate on the Union's institutional future. The Laeken summit of 2001 issued a declaration calling for more democracy, transparency and openness. It also launched the Convention on the Future of Europe, their response to the failures of successive IGCs. The Convention, chaired by the former French President Valéry Giscard d'Estaing, was composed of 105 members drawn from the national parliaments of member states and candidate countries, the European Parliament, the European Commission, and representatives of the Heads of State and Government. It met for the first time in February 2002. In July 2003, a 'Draft Treaty establishing a Constitution for Europe' was presented to the Italian Presidency. Further squabbling between the member states (who declined to allow the Convention to draft the final version of the text) dragged the negotiation process out until June 2004, when the Constitutional Treaty was accepted.

And then politics took over. A number of member states decided, often for political reasons, to ratify the document by referendum, culminating in rejections by the French and Dutch publics in May and June 2005 respectively. As if this were not bad enough, increasingly acerbic budgetary arguments broke out as the period covered by Agenda 2000 came to an end. And all this combined with concerns about the possible implications of enlargement – by ten in 2004 (and a further two in 2007).

Certainly, a mere two years later, the Heads of State and Government reached agreement on a document identical in most respects to that rejected in the Netherlands and France. Yet the tensions and bitter debates that preceded the signing of the 'Lisbon Treaty' were illustrative of the limited ability of the member states to agree on treaty reforms. And, in stark contrast to the pious wishes they had expressed at Laeken, they not only negotiated the text in secret but also pointedly refused to submit a treaty almost identical in every major respect to its ill-fated predecessor to popular ratification via referenda. So much for a more transparent and open Union brought closer to its people. The Treaty, whatever its fate, is unlikely to mark the end of political struggles over, and popular dissatisfaction with, the Union.

★

The European Council meeting of June 2005 tried to put on a brave face following the Dutch and French referenda. The assembled leaders declared that the 'European ambition, which has served us so well for over 50 years and which has allowed Europe to unite around the same vision, remains more relevant than ever'. Instructively, the *New York Times* saw things rather differently:

> The leaders of the 25 European Union nations went home after a failed two-day summit meeting in anger and in shame, as domestic politics and national interests defeated lofty notions of sacrifice and solidarity for the benefit of all… the failure of the summit meeting laid bare the deep divide within the European Union between grand but competing visions of Europe.[19]

The latter is the more convincing account. Over fifty years since its inception, the member states cannot agree on a 'vision' of European integration as the heated debates over the Reform Treaty drafted to replace the document produced by the Convention illustrated all too clearly. More importantly, they can no longer agree on much else either. Despite this, they continued to dump responsibilities on the Union without providing either the funds or institutional arrangements necessary for their effective discharge.

All the while, despite their obsession with ambitious new schemes, market creation has continued, with striking progress made in the creation of a single European economic space. The chapters that follow examine in more detail how the complex and far-reaching system of cooperation that emerged from this tangled history functions today.

3

FRAGILE UNION

O n 20 September 1988, Margaret Thatcher travelled to Belgium to deliver what was to become her most famous statement on European integration. The Bruges speech, delivered to the College of Europe, training ground for aspirant EU officials, has subsequently become an essential point of reference for Eurosceptics. 'My first guiding principle,' declared the Prime Minister, 'is this: willing and active cooperation between independent sovereign states is the best way to build a successful European Community.' On the same day, doubtless taking advantage of her absence, the Danish Prime Minister, Poul Schluter, made a speech of his own in London. He, too, was interested in the state, albeit from a very different perspective: 'The nation state,' he opined, 'was born of the industrial society, and like industrial society it is becoming outworn.'[1]

The two pronouncements were indicative of the highly polarized nature of debates over the Union. While one side advocates the creation of a quasi-federal replacement for the nation state, the other warns of its dangers, insisting that European integration is, and should remain, simply a form of traditional international cooperation.

Actually, there is far too much discussion about how the EU works. Observers and practitioners alike spend inordinate amounts of time describing decision-making processes and institutional configurations, and far less examining what the Union actually does and how well it does it. Indeed, a whole obfuscatory lexicon has been developed to describe process, involving terms such as 'Community method', 'subsidiarity', 'supranationalism', 'comitology' or 'the Lamfalussy process'. Hardly surprisingly, such intricacies are of little interest to the European public. In June 2005, the Commission stated the blindingly obvious. Citizens, it had discovered, have a 'fairly low knowledge and interest in how the EU institutions operate' yet, simultaneously, 'high expectations on delivery and policy content'.[2]

What the Union does is, without doubt, more important than how it does it. Yet process matters, if only because processes shape outcomes. If the Union is expected to perform certain tasks, the structures need to be in place to enable it to do so. And it is only by understanding how the EU operates that we will be in a position to appreciate what expectations we can legitimately have of it in terms of delivery and policy content.

All the more so in the case of the EU than of other political systems. The European Union does much of what states do. It regulates, it legislates, and its institutions are supposed to ensure implementation of its laws. Yet it does them

in very different ways from nation states. Its real uniqueness, in other ways, resides in its form rather than in its
functions.

The Union is also hugely complex. Certainly, most political systems are. Yet the historical development of the EU
has ensured that it is more so than most. The steady
increases in competence remarked on in the previous
chapter necessitated the development of different forms of
policy making in different policy sectors. Paul Magnette has
estimated that, without even considering the second and
third pillars, decision making occurs via twenty-two different legislative procedures and thirty legal instruments.[3] At
the same time, the Union has had to reconcile the sensitivities of an ever-increasing number of member states, all
anxious not only to act together, but also to preserve as
much of their own influence as possible while so doing.
Little wonder, then, that its institutions defy pithy explanation.

What they lack in clarity, however, they more than make
up for in ingenuity. The reality of the Union's institutional
system corresponds to neither the Thatcher nor the
Schluter interpretation. Its strength – and its novelty – lies
in its subtle amalgam of the powers of the member states
and its own institutions. Yet it is fragile, increasingly in
danger of erosion as states baulk at the constraints imposed
by a system they themselves created and control.

★

Much nonsense is talked about the institutions of the Union, references to a European superstate or the 'rapid accumulation of power in Brussels'[4] being prominent. The reality is far different. The EU is a weak institution, heavily, and increasingly, reliant on its constituent member states.[5]

Indicative of the ignorance characterizing appraisals of the Union was the poll carried out by the BBC's *Today* programme in December 2005. According to this, the Commission's President, José Manuel Barroso, runs Britain. Nonsense. Indeed, as we shall see, it is open to question whether he even runs the Commission. Yet it is easy to understand why the Commission in particular is so frequently and so profoundly misunderstood. It is a curious institution, both the bureaucracy of the Union and, at times, prone to act like some kind of proto-government for it.

As explained in chapter 1, institutions like the Commission are created to deal with issues that member states would not wish to entrust to their partners. States, however, do not willingly accept the existence of a higher authority in international politics. The Commission, therefore, was set up to act as a referee rather than as a team captain. And, like all referees, its effectiveness depends on a reputation for impartiality.

This impartiality is symbolized in the 'solemn undertaking' given by Commissioners on taking office that they will 'neither seek nor take instructions from any government or any other body'. Reality is, of course, more complex. It makes sense for Commissioners to be in close contact with the governments to whom they will be proposing legislation and whose implementation of that legislation they will monitor. And member states have always tried to appoint reliable representatives of national positions as Commissioners, although it is not always easy for them to do so. Lord Cockfield, appointed by Mrs Thatcher, was denied a second term by her, as she felt he had 'gone native' in Brussels.

In practice, different Commissioners have acted in different ways, partly at least as a function of the incentives confronting them. Career paths provide one clue. The UK has traditionally appointed individuals at the end of their political careers. Consequently, although they might share the views of their government (no one need cajole a Leon Brittan or a Peter Mandelson into supporting free trade), there is little to make them claim to do so when they do not. In contrast, some French Commissioners have potentially bright political futures in Paris ahead of them. Claude Cheysson became Foreign Minister after his stint in Brussels, and Raymond Barre went on to be Prime Minister and to stand for the Presidency. Many believed Jacques Delors would do the same. Thus, when he publicly rebuked the Agriculture Commissioner, Ray MacSharry, for making too many concessions to the Americans over agricultural subsidies, this was interpreted by *The Economist* as the opening salvo of his campaign to become the next French President (farmers are, of course, a crucial constituency in French elections).[6] Commission independence tends to pale into insignificance when measured against the glittering prize of high office at home. Then again, at least Delors had the decency to hang around. Romano Prodi disappeared from Brussels during much of the last year of his tenure, so intent was he on running his Italian election campaign. Louis Michel took unpaid leave from the trivia of running the Commission's development portfolio to pursue his ambition of a return to Belgian politics.

The balancing act performed by Commissioners has been an aspect of European integration since its inception. And the concept of their independence has taken several blows in recent years. Increasingly, and particularly during negotiations at Nice and during the Convention, national Commissioners have been used as bargaining chips in negotiations over institutional reform, to the point where a former French Prime Minister could state baldly that 'I know Commissioners do not represent their own countries but represent the greater good of Europe as a whole, but we all know that is just window dressing and that Commissioners are always interested in promoting the interests of the countries that sent them to Brussels.'[7] So much for the impartiality of the referee.

Changing attitudes towards the Commission date from the time of Jacques Delors, since when member states have become increasingly wary of it. One reason was fear about the excessive ambitions for it that he displayed. Another was the increasing importance for them of what the Commission does in terms of regulating and enforcing the single market. In the early years of European integration, when de Gaulle's Foreign Minister informed him that Paris had to find 300 officials to make up the French complement in the nascent Commission, his response was 'send the most stupid'. No longer.

For many years now, national influences have pervaded the Commission. The Mediterranean states have always dominated those Directorates General charged with running the structural funds, while DG Competition has a reputation as a home for British and German competition lawyers. A Frenchman (not the same one) headed DG Agriculture from 1958 to 1999. Junior officials are particularly influential in that Commission proposals tend to resemble very closely the original drafts drawn up by them. According to some estimates, 80 per cent of the original draft legislation survives in the final text adopted by the Council. Life becomes much easier for a national government if that junior official can be trusted to produce an acceptable proposal in the first place. Consequently, capitals increasingly attempt to place 'their' people at all levels of the institution; and to ensure loyalty, several of them seem quite taken with the idea of sending short-term secondees, whose incentives to remain 'loyal' to their home administration are obvious.

Increasingly subverted from within, Commission independence is also being challenged from without. For a variety of reasons, member states have colluded in allowing the European Parliament enhanced power over the appointment of its President. Partly, this is a result of their incompetence. The current procedure, whereby they agree on a candidate 'by common accord' tends to lead to selection of the least offensive rather than necessarily most able candidate (not, admittedly, the only selection process that works in this way). Consequently, it is easy to argue that any alternative system would represent an improvement.

Moreover, politicians find it hard to argue publicly against giving more power to a political institution that looks, and to an extent acts, like any parliament (though they are in private often less than charitable about it). As pointed out in chapter 1, political leaders are more interested in talking about democracy than liberal democracy, and are thus reluctant to be seen to be 'opposing democracy'.

Incompetence and cowardice have led to a situation in which the EP has secured for itself at least an informal right to approve the Commission as a whole before it formally takes office. It also led member states to agree to a provision in the Lisbon Treaty whereby the Commission President would be elected by the European Parliament.

Such schemes are based on a fundamental misapprehension of the nature and purpose of the Community institutions. Elections would serve to lower, not increase, trust in the Commission. Not merely because it has been selected by a potentially partisan majority, but also because there will always be the lingering suspicion that its actions once in office will be about re-election rather than impartial refereeing. The institution would thus be subject to precisely the kinds of time inconsistency problems that lead national politicians to delegate tasks to non-elected institutions in the first place. As explained in chapter 1, all this goes against the very point of having a Commission at all.

Such trends have already begun to subvert trust in Commission impartiality. It is illuminating that the French daily *Le Figaro* was moved to assert that a November 2005 reshuffle of senior administrators 'shows how far France has lost influence in Brussels'. It matters, in other words, if the Hunt Tsar is seen to be a particularly good friend of one of the hunters. Nation states are suspicious enough of inter-national institutions without needing additional reasons for distrust. Plans to introduce ideological bias via election, or, as Commissioner Günter Verheugen has suggested, depriv-ing small member states of their Commissioners would merely provide such reasons.

Prone to ever more member state interference, the Commission has also become a victim of its own success. Again, the roots of this can be traced to the Presidency of Delors. Under him, the institution focused on 'building Europe' rather than on making the EC/EU function effec-tively. Responsible for ever more tasks entrusted to it by the member states, the Commission came to regard the volume of work done as a more accurate measure of its standing than how well it carried out its tasks.[8]

Yet as anyone – particularly a recipient of EU research funding – knows only too well, managing projects is often far more onerous than getting approval for them in the first place. The Commission lacks the organizational capacities necessary for it to carry out its portfolio of tasks. In 1998, the Santer Commission was accused of fraud and mis-management, and a Group of Wise Men was established to look into these allegations. Their report pulled no punches, referring scathingly to a situation 'tantamount to an admission of a loss of control by the political authorities over the administration they are supposed to be running' and adding, for good measure, that 'it was becoming difficult to find anyone who has even the slightest sense of responsibility.'

Such failings can only partly be attributed to the Commission itself. It is the member states, after all, who continue to view staffing questions in terms of a need to match 'flags to posts', thereby limiting the development of a culture of merit. They also control the purse strings. The Commission is not the bloated bureaucratic structure that so many believe it to be. While significantly bigger than the secretariats of either the Association of South-East Asian Nations (ASEAN) or the South American trade pact MER-CUSOR, it is much smaller than national administrations. There are a mere 30,000 EU officials in total, of whom about 20,000 work for the Commission. As we saw in chapter 1, by 1985, the British central government contained within it over a million civil servants. The budgetary comparison is every bit as striking. The 2004 administrative budget of the European Commission was smaller than that of the Mayor of London (which stood at £2.8 billion, or just over €4 billion). While national bureaucracies eat up, on average, between 23 and 28 per cent of national budgets, the EU institutions together consume a mere 5.5 per cent of a far smaller budget. Nevertheless, and despite the increasing demands placed upon the institution by the 2004 enlargement, EU Finance Ministers in July 2006 approved radical cuts in the Commission staff budget, amounting to an 8.5 per cent reduction in its staff.

Speaking of enlargement, it has become common in EU jargon to distinguish between widening – enlargement – and 'deepening' – less well defined, but generally taken to mean either an expansion in EU competence or greater powers for the central institutions. The distinction, however, is a false one, and the Commission is often the loser as a result. Widening involves deepening. The very process of enlargement involves the Commission in the onerous task of ensuring respect for the EU rule book on the part of aspirant members. Once they have joined, it must police the new member states as well, ensuring their continued compliance. Policing nation states is not an easy task. Policing ever more of them with ever scarcer resources is more difficult still. And this while the Commission has to reform itself internally in order to allow for appointments to its ranks from among the new entrants. Obsessed with the implications of enlargement for their relative weight within the Council or their own pet policy concerns, member states have tended to overlook this implication of the process.

The other pillar of the Union's 'supranational' system is the European Court of Justice (ECJ). It makes little sense to pass laws if there exists no court to interpret and enforce them. And the ECJ has, as we have seen, been hugely influential in transforming the Community legal order. The doctrines of supremacy and direct effect have no analogue in international relations. And the ingenuity of the EC legal system does not stop there. The so-called preliminary ruling procedure (under which the ECJ can rule on any aspect of EC law referred to it by a national court) has been instrumental in the development of this legal order. The procedure has become an ingenious means of compensating for the institutional weakness of a court which, unlike the US Supreme Court, has no physical presence on the territories of the states. National courts refer queries – often brought by private citizens – to the ECJ, which rules on them. It then falls to the national courts to enforce the decision within their territories. National courts, in other words, have been coopted into the EC system.

The Court is not the target of the kinds of pressures from member states to which the Commission has increasingly been subject. Judges are appointed to a six-year renewable term. Because the Court deliberates in secret, national governments have no way of knowing with any certainty how 'their' justices have acted. And despite periodic dissatisfaction with the Court, national governments have proved reluctant to curtail its authority.

Yet the court must act within constraints. Even the core principle of supremacy, such a watershed in the development of the Community, is not absolute. It has not been unequivocally accepted by national constitutional courts, but is, rather, tolerated by them. And only up to a point. German and Italian courts have, for instance, questioned the principle because of the lack of a bill of fundamental rights within the EU Treaty. The ECJ subsequently asserted that the Community did indeed recognize the fundamental rights inspired by those constitutional traditions common to the member states, leading to qualified acceptance of the doctrine by those courts. They were, in effect, accepting supremacy to the extent that it was legitimized by member states themselves. The Community legal system presided over by the ECJ is not, then, hierarchical or self-referential. Rather, it is one intertwined with the law of the member states.

And the Court has had to be sensitive to the sensibilities of those states in interpreting the law. Twenty-five years ago, a prominent legal scholar explained its success in the following terms: 'Tucked away in the fairyland Duchy of Luxembourg and blessed, until recently, with benign neglect by the powers that be and the mass media, the Court of Justice of the European Communities has fashioned a constitutional framework for a federal-type Europe.'[9] Subsequent to this, as we have seen, the scope of integration has expanded enormously and the Court has intervened in high-profile cases dealing with sensitive aspects of national political life ranging from health care to taxation (both are discussed in chapter 4). As it intrudes on national prerogatives in this way, two things happen. First, national governments pay more attention to it, and benign neglect is transformed into watchfulness. Governments that initially did not bother now set down more and more observations in ongoing ECJ cases to make their positions known.[10]

Second, the Court becomes a target for political attack. The Austrian Chancellor, Wolfgang Schüssel, dismayed by an

ECJ judgment that obliged Austria to open its medical schools fully to German students (who already accounted for more than half the applicants to some colleges), launched just such an attack at the start of the Austrian Presidency in 2006, urging the Court to 'pay more heed to public opinion and to refrain from handing down heavy-handed judgments'.[11] Member states can also retaliate in more practical ways. The Barber Protocol, appended to the Maastricht Treaty, limited the retroactive applicability of an ECJ ruling on gender equality for occupational pensions. It was clearly an attempt to limit the impact of the Court. Barber, certainly, was exceptional. Treaty changes require unanimity, and it is difficult indeed to find a Court decision with which not a single member state agrees. Nevertheless, it served to send a warning signal: go too far, and we will react.

If the two appointed supranational institutions are more sensitive to member state opinion than is often assumed, the elected one is more effective than frequently thought. The European Parliament is the world's only directly elected transnational parliament. It has seen its powers rise dramatically over the course of the last twenty years or so, not least because governments have sought to reassure their electorates that the EU system is, in fact, democratic. It now enjoys co-legislative status with the Council of Ministers over most areas related to the single market and the composition of the EU budget.

The EP is an institution that is often unfairly maligned for shortcomings that lie outside its control. Take the ongoing saga about its location. It has two homes, and moves from Brussels to Strasbourg every month at an estimated annual cost of some €200 million. This situation has long been a cause of concern and recently was the object of a one-million signature online petition organized by a Swedish MEP. Yet it remains unchanged and will continue to do so for one simple reason. The French government insists on the maintenance of Strasbourg as a parliamentary seat and unanimity between member states is necessary for this to change. The strength of French opposition is such that, despite the petition, the Austrian Presidency simply refused to put the issue on the agenda of the June 2006 European Council meeting.

In fact, and again contrary to what many assume, the EP is, in some ways, a highly effective legislature. Many MEPs are extremely competent in their areas of expertise, and the various specialist parliamentary committees often produce impressive reports on, and propose telling amendments to, draft legislation. And unlike many national parliaments, dominated by the ruling party and hence little more than cheerleaders for government-sponsored legislation, it wields a real influence over legislation, proving willing to reject drafts or amend them significantly.

Yet the Parliament nevertheless fails to live up to the scale of its own ambitions. Certainly, it is easy to appreciate the need for some kind of democratic control over decisions that member states vote on by qualified majority. Without it, citizens whose governments found themselves outvoted in the Council might complain of a lack of effective voice in proceedings. Yet many in the institution are not satisfied with this. A constant quest for increasing authority within the Union thus often underlies its actions. In October 2006, its budgetary committee voted to slash the budget for the Common Foreign and Security Policy (CFSP) simply to underline its dissatisfaction with its lack of control over how the money would be spent. The EP is an institution whose *raison d'être* depends on movement towards an ever more integrated political union; consequently it worries as much about constantly driving forward the process of integration as it does about its primary task of legislative scrutiny.[12]

Perhaps most damningly of all, there are good reasons to doubt whether the Parliament enjoys the democratic credentials to justify even its current role, let alone its pretensions. MEPs are elected from national party lists in national constituencies, via nationally organized elections generally based around debates over national issues. The 'European' nature of their mandate is thus sketchy at best, with steadily decreasing turnout at EP elections serving merely to cast further doubt upon their claim to legitimacy. The lack of mandate directly challenges the Parliament's claims to be able to act as the mouthpiece of the 'European people' in Brussels, as events have underlined:

> The rejection of the constitution in the French and Dutch referendums has cruelly exposed the fantasy that the European Parliament is the answer to the disconnect between political elites and ordinary citizens. The parliament – including French and Dutch

MEPs – voted overwhelmingly to approve the EU constitution, only to find that the voters seemed to disagree.[13]

Differences in turnout were also revealing. That for the 2004 European elections in France had been 43 per cent, in contrast to the 70 per cent that voted in the referendum. For the Netherlands, the equivalent figures were 39 and 63 per cent.[14] And while voters are reluctant to vote, MEPs themselves have done their cause no good by their own failure to turn up at work (a trait, admittedly, they share with many national counterparts). Turnout at sessions is notoriously low: a paltry 82 of the 732 members attended a vote calling for the closure of Guantanamo Bay. For all the fuss made about holding the Commission to account, Barroso presented his 2006 work programme in front of a chamber containing more representatives from the Commission than MEPs.[15]

It is also arguable that the more influential the EP becomes, the less it will be allowed by the member states to act like a 'normal' parliament. Just as in the case of the Commission, increasing powers foster a desire for enhanced control. The adoption by the British Labour Party of a list system for the selection of MEPs was, partly at least, an attempt to exercise central control over who gets to go to Brussels (and Strasbourg). And national administrations now spend far more time than ever lobbying 'their' MEPs. With some success. In the vote over the appointment of Barroso as Commission President, the Spanish socialists voted against the socialist group in the EP because of a deal between their government and its partners, whereby Spain was given the post of High Representative for Foreign Policy in return for its support for the Portuguese presidential candidate.[16]

Which tawdry tale brings us to the member states themselves. The Council of Ministers makes up the final major piece of this complicated institutional jigsaw. While, on the one hand, a traditional interstate negotiating forum, it is a highly complex institution, divided horizontally into nine different sectoral formations, each responsible for decisions in its own area of expertise, and vertically between the ministerial councils themselves and a series of committees and working groups made up of officials from the member states.

This structure impinges on the way the institution works. Its sectoral groupings can appear like a series of unconnected 'silos', each working in its own area without reference to the others. Farmers have long profited from the fact that agriculture remains the preserve of the Special Committee on Agriculture, whose workings are dominated by friends of the agricultural sector.

The workings and strategic position of the Council are instructive. For all the ingenuity of the EU system, the fact that states acting in the Council reserved the right to react to Commission legislative proposals illustrated a desire to retain ultimate control over what the Union does. Moreover, for all the fuss made about majority voting, and despite the fact that successive treaty revisions have increased the range of issues to which it applies, consensus has remained its rule of thumb. Estimates suggest that only around 10 per cent of decisions are arrived at via a formal vote, while the *Financial Times* (13 September 1994) claimed that, between 1989 and 1993, only 91 single market decisions out of 233 were adopted by qualified majority.

Even on those occasions when it is used, it is worth bearing in mind that the threshold for a qualified majority is set remarkably high. Indeed, even for routine legislative decisions on the single market, the requirement is for a majority equivalent to that required in some states to pass a constitutional amendment. Nothing can be imposed against the wishes of the largest four member states, while they, in turn, cannot push something through without the support of at least seven of their partners. Indeed, in order to ensure against the tyranny of the 'bigs', current voting arrangements – set down under the 2000 Nice Treaty – are relatively population-insensitive, with Germany (population 82 million) having 29 votes, while Luxembourg (population 450,000) has 4.

Sovereign states, in other words, are sensitive about being outvoted when law is being made, and reluctant to force their partners against the wall. For instance, there have only ever been four ECJ judgments against member states stemming from cases brought by other member states. This reflects, in part, a kind of 'there but for the grace of God' reflex. It also reflects the fact that embittered governments enjoy plenty of opportunities to seek revenge. Italy on one occasion prevented a vote on sanctions against

Belarus in retaliation against states such as Germany and the UK which had blocked the imposition of tariffs on Chinese imports.

Just as the increasing salience of European integration and successive enlargements have had implications for the Commission, so too have they affected the workings of the Council. The most obvious manifestation of the changing dynamics of interstate negotiation has been the emergence of potentially damaging divisions between competing 'clubs'.

Growing tensions between large and small member states came to prominence during the successive IGCs at the end of the last decade. Larger member states felt increasing unease about an Eastern enlargement that brought in numerous 'smalls'. This had implications for all the institutions. Giscard d'Estaing described as 'grotesque' a situation in which large member states enjoyed the same representation (*sic*) in the Commission as a Baltic nation, while former French Prime Minister Édouard Balladur pointed out the anomaly that, while a German MEP represents 800,000 people, the figure for some small member states is 30–40,000.[17] In terms of the Council itself, such concerns found expression in the Constitutional Treaty, which undertook a significant re-weighting of votes to place more emphasis on population, an issue taken up again in the Lisbon Treaty.

More substantively, the small member states were, at the same time, more and more alarmed by what they saw as a tendency on the part of their larger partners to throw their weight around. The so-called G6 – established as the G5 in 2003 – brings together Justice Ministers from France, Germany, Italy, Poland (since 2004), Spain and the UK two or three times a year. While no formal decisions are taken, the meetings help to set the EU agenda. Its activities have led the House of Lords EU committee to express concern about its lack of transparency and to caution that it 'should not try to ride rough-shod over the 19 smaller member states'.[18]

In the foreign policy field, a number of member states have expressed at least private dissatisfaction with the secretive handling by France, Germany and the UK of their ongoing negotiations with Iran over its nuclear ambitions. On one occasion, twenty-two of the twenty-five Foreign Ministers were not allowed to see a 'top secret' report produced by Tehran to explain its position. Perhaps this was justifiable, given the sensitivity of the issue at hand. Infinitely less so was the way in which France and Germany systematically destroyed the Stability and Growth Pact. Designed (by Germany) to ensure fiscal discipline on the part of eurozone members, the Pact died in 2003 when the two states not only breached its terms, but then proceeded to persuade their partners that they should not be punished (see chapter 5). Resulting concerns that the Union was based on one rule for France and Germany, and another for the rest, played a significant role in shifting Dutch public opinion against the Constitutional Treaty.

Partly reinforcing, partly cutting across this split (depending really on the mood in Poland on any particular day), is that pitting new, particularly Central and Eastern European, member states against their Western partners. The beginnings of resentment predated accession, and were hardly unreasonable. Chirac referred during the Iraq crisis to the candidate countries as 'badly brought up' and, typically unsubtly, threatened that France could block their accession if they continued to disagree with him. Hardly reassuring for the newcomers.

They had been warned. Subsequent to accession, their worst fears about second-class status have come close to being realized. Supposed 'technical' problems resulted in continued delays to their inclusion in the Schengen area (from which frontier controls have been removed), while numerous member states have imposed restrictions on the mobility of Central and East European workers. Most glaringly, several of the new entrants, including Poland, the Czech Republic and Slovakia, supported the Lithuanians in demanding clarification of the inflation criteria used to keep the latter out of the eurozone. The proximate cause was that the country had missed the target by a mere 0.07 per cent. Leaving aside the asinine nature of the rules, their apparent arbitrariness, or the way they had so systematically been bent when decisions about the original composition of the eurozone had been made, the decision was all the more galling coming, as it did, so soon after France and Germany had flouted EU fiscal rules with impunity. Little wonder, then, that some suspected Lithuania's exclusion to have been an example of discrimination against a new member state.

If the foregoing has not served to underline the ubiquitous, entrenched and pervasive influence of the member
states over the system, we now turn to the institution at the
apex of the EU institutional system – the European Council
composed of their Heads of State and Government.[19] Since
its creation in 1974, this has been responsible for virtually
all major decisions associated with the Union, from acceptance of the single market programme to the launch of the
euro, to the development of the European Security and
Defence Policy. Given its rarefied membership, it is
uniquely placed not only to provide leadership but also to
unblock the Council system when disputes arise over
matters that the ministers in the various sectoral councils
find difficult to resolve.

The impact of the European Council has increased significantly in recent years. It now plays a role in economic
policy through its involvement in the implementation of
the Lisbon agenda. Its members take an active interest in
new and high-profile policy domains such as defence and
internal security. Also of note is the prevalence of intergovernmental conferences, all of which terminate in a summit
meeting at which the details of treaty changes are thrashed
out. Speaking at the opening session of the 1985 intergovernmental conference that was to negotiate the Single
European Act, Delors remarked that 'conferences like this
one are not convened every five or ten years. There may
not be another one between now and 2000.'[20] In fact, as we
have seen, there were a further three, increasing the role of
the European Council in the affairs of the EU.

For all its growing profile, however, the European Council is not necessarily effective. Rather than providing the strategic leadership they are uniquely well positioned to supply, its members often resort to potentially damaging short-term fixes to resolve current policy problems. In September 2006, anxious to avoid domestic repercussions and potentially huge cost (see chapter 4), Tony Blair offered Romano Prodi support for anti-dumping duties on cheap Chinese and Vietnamese shoes in return for the latter's support over the working time directive. Free trade sacrificed on the altar of political expediency. At Copenhagen in December 2002, Greece threatened to veto the forthcoming enlargement if Cyprus was not allowed to join. France insisted on the enshrining of Strasbourg as part-time home for the European Parliament in the Maastricht Treaty.

Given the structure of meetings – they last only a couple of days – decisions with long-term consequences are often taken at the last minute. Indeed, obstructing discussion has become something of an art form. The British presented their December 2005 budgetary proposal – setting the EU budget for a seven-year period – only ten days before the meeting at which agreement had to be reached. An accord was finally reached at 2 a.m. Similarly, the German Presidency gave its partners only two days to consider the draft declaration prepared to mark the fiftieth anniversary of the Treaty of Rome.

And pettiness, egos and narrow national obsessions are never far from the surface. The unsatisfactory nature of the institution's selection of Commission Presidents has already been remarked upon. Meanwhile, at a 2003 summit meant to discus Iraq, Berlusconi put Italian milk quotas on the agenda. The December 2005 summit saw angry arguments about the location of the new EU Food Safety Authority, with the same Italian Prime Minister injecting his own unique perspective: 'Finns don't even know what prosciutto is' (prompting the Finnish MEP Lasse Lehtinen, anxious to maintain the high standard of debate, to retort that Berlusconi's recent facelift 'may have affected his brain').

The reassertion of member state control over the EU system, therefore, has hardly been a recipe for enhanced effectiveness. Member states have, by their actions, called into question the rule of law and placed the issue of national representation in the institutions above that of the overall effectiveness of the system. International institutions serve to engender and entrench reciprocity. Yet reciprocity is based on trust. Recent years have seen a gradual erosion of trust, both between member states in an increasingly factionalized Council, and between them and the supranational institutions, most notably the Commission. And as this in turn has led them to place increased constraints on that institution, the prospects of effective negotiations in the Council itself diminish. As the Commission's first President, Walter Hallstein, pointed out, the institution was intended to provide a 'constant reminder of a Community interest transcending the interest of each of the participants', and to do so by playing the role of 'honest broker'.[21] A tapped-up, distrusted, under-resourced and over-committed Hunt Tsar will ultimately benefit none of the hunters.

★

Central to the workings of the European Community is the 'Community method', which applies to most single market legislation (and will, under the Lisbon Treaty, be used for certain aspects of asylum and immigration policies as well).

It is in the Community method that we see the subtle blending of Community and member states that has allowed for such striking progress to be made in market creation. Legislation is proposed by the European Commission, voted on by the member states and the European Parliament, and implemented and enforced by the Commission and the European Court of Justice. The Commission's right to propose legislation ensures that no member state can clog the system with its own pet projects, and that 'European' considerations determine the legislative agenda.

Member states, however, vote on every piece of legislation and so ultimately have a lock on what becomes law. Yet because they sometimes do so on the basis of a majority vote, the parliament acts as a democratic safety net. And the two 'supranational' institutions – the Court and the Commission – impartially ensure (in theory at least) that the law as passed is properly implemented and enforced.

Lawmaking in the Union is a complicated business. Necessarily so, as it involves reconciling not only the member states but also other actors, most notably an increasingly assertive European Parliament. Little surprise, then, that the process is a slow one. It can take years for the member states to agree on a Commission legislative proposal. Thereafter, it often requires complex negotiations to satisfy both the requisite number of member states and the Parliament. One consequence is the production of extremely complicated legislation. The Registration, Evaluation and Authorization of Chemicals (REACH) directive, following a tortuous negotiation process involving serial amendments, eventually stretched to some one thousand pages (itself a recipe for uncertainty as it becomes harder to predict precise outcomes, particularly if the Court is called on to rule on vague texts).

Another oft-criticized feature of EC lawmaking concerns the amount of law that is produced. Chancellor Merkel of Germany called in May 2006 for the abolition of a quarter of existing legislation. The previous October, the Commission had launched a drive to scrap or simplify more than 1,500 pieces of legislation, having announced the previous month its intention to scrap sixty-eight draft laws. The fact that this was not the first such attempt should warn us, however, that law scrapping is harder than lawmaking. Between 1995 and 1999, the Santer Commission had operated under the slogan 'do less better'. In 2002, as part of the implementation of the Lisbon Strategy, the Prodi Commission had issued its own better-regulation action plan.

The problem, as ever, lies with the member states themselves. Vague and complex legislation is often a necessary outcome of negotiations in the Council during which governments insist on opt-outs, derogations and recognition of their own specific circumstances. The volume of EC legislation owes much to their desire to ensure that their own regulatory traditions are reflected on the EU statute book. That a directive of December 2001 decreed that 'tomatoes, the edible parts of rhubarb stalks, carrots, sweet potatoes, cucumbers, pumpkins, melons and water-melons are considered to be fruit' owed more to Portuguese jam-making traditions than to insidious imperialistic designs on the part of the Commission. Member states just cannot help themselves.

The decision to pass a law, moreover, represents only the first part of the story of public policy. Because of the need to secure agreement in the Council, member states often resort to passing framework legislation that requires significant 'filling in' prior to coming into force. The way they do this bears eloquent testimony to their creativeness in inventing ever more ways to control the system. They have even coined a word – 'comitology' – to put off people who might express an interest in how the system works.

Basically, it works like this. Committees of experts from the member states get together with the Commission to decide on the technical details of a broad piece of legislation. The Commission generally needs the approval of all of these before it can begin implementation. If this is not forthcoming, the measure is referred back to the Council (so member states enjoy a unanimity lock). Member states can thus get down to the real business of squabbling over the spoils in private. And not only is the Commission's role more limited than in the legislative phase, but comitology effectively sidelines a Parliament which, under the treaties, enjoys co-legislative status in discussions of the budget (without any embarrassing need to explain to publics why this is happening).

Once finalized, legislation must be implemented. Here too, member states have created a specific kind of law which maximizes their freedom of manoeuvre. The most common form of law produced by the EC is the directive. The crucial distinguishing feature of these legal instruments is that they merely specify the objectives to be achieved, rather than the detailed means by which they will be. Implementation, therefore, demands that they be 'transposed' into national laws specifying how the agreed-upon objectives will be achieved.

Some member states seem willing to sign up to anything in Brussels and then add it to the 'pending' pile (Greece has often been considered to be one such state). Perhaps the Internal Market Commissioner, Charlie McCreevy, was sincere in saying he took 'the old-fashioned view that a minister's signature on a directive should be a firm commitment, not a vague aspiration'.[22] Not all ministers share his opinion, however. In 2006, the Commission threatened legal action against nineteen of the twenty-five member states who had failed to transpose a 2004 directive setting minimum standards for refugee status. In 2002 the Commission had 1,500 infringement proceedings open against member states for failing to apply directives fully. Equally worrying, it found that the performance of the old member states was worse in terms of transposition than that of the new entrants.

It should be noted here that one of the reasons for

member state hesitation concerning the 'better regulation' initiative they themselves insist upon publicly is a fear that 'better' might be taken by some nefarious eurocrats to imply 'more effective'. Rationalization of the statute book could involve the replacement of directives, and the leeway they provide to even those states which transpose them, with regulations, which remove such discretion, ensuring uniform rules and immediate application.

Even once transposition has occurred, the Community faces the challenge of ensuring prompt and uniform implementation. The preliminary reference procedure here provides a useful means of mobilizing individuals in defence of the Community legal order. Yet the EU institutions themselves lack the resources fully to enforce the law in all twenty-seven member states. These latter are, moreover, ingenious when it comes to finding ways of avoiding their commitments. In 1979, when required by EU law to declare its bathing beaches to the Commission, the UK declared merely twenty-seven – compared with 8,000 in the rest of EU and thirty-nine in landlocked Luxembourg.[23] Not that Britain is alone in its perfidy. The Commission reported in April 2006 that 7,000 bathing sites in eleven countries had been removed from lists, with France delisting some 50 per cent of its freshwater sites (perhaps they have evaporated).

Even once a transgression is identified, forcing a state to obey the law is not easy. In 1994, Italy passed a privatization law that was declared illegal by the ECJ in March 2000. Subsequently, it has been repeatedly amended, though never quite to the satisfaction of the Commission, which, in

October 2005 – almost ten years after the passage of the original Act – was forced to issue another caution. Within a state, an individual would be imprisoned, fined or both for such crass defiance. Law and politics between states, however, are different. Certainly, there is an infringement process. And fines have been imposed. In July 2000, the Greek government was the first to be fined – €20,000 per day. The largest fine, imposed by the ECJ in a judgment of 12 July 2005, led to France being ordered to pay a penalty payment of €57,761,250 for each period of six months it continued to flout EU rules on fisheries, along with a lump sum of €20 million.

Yet fines are very rare, with only a handful of cases getting that far. Hardly surprising, as the procedure leading to their imposition is complex. Stage one involves negotiations between the Commission and the member state concerned. The Commission can then, if necessary, refer the case to the ECJ. If the state fails to comply with the court ruling, the Commission can return to the Court and request the imposition of sanctions. While providing states with countless opportunities to avoid punishment, the process is also painfully slow. The first ruling in the saga that led to the above fine being imposed on France for allowing undersized fish to be sold was handed down in 1991.

★

The Community method aside, the other striking institutional innovation undertaken by the Union concerns the arrangements in place for managing the single currency. Uniquely, monetary policy is highly centralized in the hands of the European Central Bank (ECB), while fiscal and political authority is dispersed among the member states.

For the Germans at Maastricht, the non-negotiable pay-off for scrapping the Deutschmark was the adoption at European level of the German monetary policy model. Consequently, the treaty lays down the principle of formal independence of the ECB, which is expressly forbidden from taking instructions from any EU government or institution. It is also legally separate from the other EU institutions, and so responsible for setting its own personnel policies and procedures. ECB independence is extreme by any standard. In pre-unification Germany, the Bundesbank could be overruled, albeit by a large majority of elected representatives in the Bundestag. Similarly the US Congress has the right to revise the statutes of the Federal Reserve. Not only is the ECB formally independent of political authority, but the EU lacks any obvious governmental authority to limit this independence. Interestingly, the 1970 Werner Report, which first proposed the move to Economic and Monetary Union, recommended an increase in the powers of the European Parliament to compensate for the loss of national political authority over monetary affairs. By the time of Maastricht, member states were sufficiently wary not to empower the Parliament in this way.

ECB independence is implemented via the independence of its President and Executive Board, all appointed by the European Council for eight-year, non-renewable terms.

Again the treaty explicitly stipulates that these individuals are not representatives of their home countries. The Governing Council, composed of the Executive Board and the Governors of the national Central Banks, takes decisions for the Bank by simple majority vote. The secrecy in which it holds its discussions (unlike the Bank of England, it publishes no minutes) is a deliberate attempt to ensure its insulation from political pressure.

Yet, as we saw in our discussion of the European Commission, independence means different things to different people. In May 1998 Jacques Chirac made clear that, for him at least, it meant having a Frenchman in charge. A shoddy compromise meant that Jean-Claude Trichet would take over as ECB President after four years of (Dutchman) Wim Duisenberg's eight-year term. The furious dispute over the Presidency was emblematic of the difficulties involved in getting states to accept the principle of truly independent international institutions in a sector as vital as monetary policy (even if Chirac's strategy was to backfire spectacularly, in that Trichet has gone on to become something of a *bête noire* of the French political class).

Nor was France alone in seeking exceptional influence. It became clear in 2006, when membership of the Executive Board came up for renewal, that the four largest eurozone countries wanted special treatment. Bluntly put, they expected to occupy four of the six slots as of right, explicit treaty stipulations that board members are not to be country representatives notwithstanding. Again, and much as in the case of the Commission, recognition of the importance of independence is tempered by member states wanting to get away with what they can.

★

Institutional arrangements for the single market and monetary policy represent the real innovations in the EU institutional system. In other areas, member states have proven far less willing, whatever functional incentives there might be, to allow independent institutions to interfere with their desire for control.

This holds true even in supposedly core areas of European integration. Agriculture was the first common policy, and is distinguishable from other policy areas in that the Common Agricultural Policy (CAP) has completely replaced national policies. Yet the CAP represents little more than the sum of its national parts. The Council of Ministers is responsible for taking key decisions – usually by consensus – in the silo that is the Special Committee on Agriculture. While on paper the Commission enjoys significant authority, it has to consult with a dense web of committees comprising representatives of the member states. And the European Parliament – remarkably given the budgetary implications of the policy – remains excluded.

Member states have used their influence over agricultural policies to develop these in such a way as to enhance their control still further. They decided, at the Berlin European Council of March 1999, on the creation of 'national envelopes' for spending in the beef and milk sectors, thereby increasing the flexibility they enjoy in deciding on how to disburse funds. A 2003 reform provided them with still more when allocating cash, in that it allowed for gross national payments, leaving national capitals with a large amount of discretion in implementing the new spending regime. We see here the inherent tension between a desire for control and the achievement of effective policy outcomes, in that once 'payments are broken down by member states, there is no longer a pan-European rationale for distributing CAP expenditure. Instead, the CAP becomes a mechanism for explicit inter-country transfers.'[24]

Member states have also increasingly created a role for themselves at EU level when it comes to economic policy more generally. The Lisbon Agenda (of which more in chapter 5) in one sense marks the involvement of the EU in all areas of economic activity. Yet the way in which it goes about this is instructive. The so-called 'Open Method of Coordination' stresses benchmarking and systematic comparison between various national practices. Yet the member states are not formally constrained in any way, with EU activity in areas such as employment based on highly decentralized, non-enforceable cooperation. And even as regards (limited) Commission involvement in monitoring member state performance, not only is it reliant for this on data provided by the national capitals themselves, but it is hard to see why it would have an incentive to be openly critical and thereby risk irritating governments on whose support it is reliant for progress in more central areas such as market creation.

The Commission's role is still more limited in the two intergovernmental 'pillars'. While it participates in the Common Foreign and Security Policy (CFSP), the member states retain a tight grip on the European Security and Defence Policy (ESDP). Both CFSP and ESDP are run by the member states on the basis of unanimity. Certainly, this makes for some incoherence. The Commission has, over the years, developed significant experience of dealing with technical, and particularly financial, aspects of foreign and security policy. Coordination between the Council and Commission is thus crucial in order that the Union play its role to the full. At present, this implies cooperation between the 'High Representative for Foreign Policy' (Javier Solana) and the Commissioner for External Relations. Under the terms of the Lisbon Treaty, a new 'High Representative of the Union for Foreign Affairs and Security Policy' would be both based in the Council and a Vice-President of the Commission. The detailed implications of the scheme need not trouble us. But it is worth pointing out that the idea underlines the increasing contempt in which member states hold the notion of Commission independence. How the unfortunate selected for the post is meant to reconcile his oath of independence with his mandate to work for the Council is anyone's guess.

The area of Justice and Home Affairs (JHA) is somewhat more complex. On the one hand, since the introduction of the pillar system, certain aspects of JHA – asylum, immigration, border controls and judicial cooperation in civil matters – have been moved into the first (EC) pillar, with police and judicial cooperation in criminal matters remaining in the intergovernmental third pillar. If only things were this simple. Desperate to reconcile their desire for efficiency (hence moving things into the first pillar and opening the possibility of voting by majority) with that for control, the member states placed unique limits on access to the European Court of Justice for matters pertaining to immigration, asylum and visas. Only courts of last resort can refer queries to the EU Court, meaning citizens have to exhaust all national legal possibilities beforehand. In what is left of the third pillar, the right is even more restricted.

★

Explaining the EU in a short book is a daunting enough task without compounding the problem by trying to examine the institutional failings of the member states themselves. This section will, of necessity, be short. Yet it nevertheless is crucial. The European Union, far from representing some kind of artificial construct separate from its constituent member states, is, in reality, a tool created and dominated by them.

Which means that the way the Union works and the impact of what it does are dependent on the way member states deal with it. This is perhaps clearest in administrative terms. We've seen how the Union depends on the member states for the implementation of its laws. And problems with implementation are often down to administrative inefficiency rather than a lack of political will (though a lack of such will can play its part). The flip side of the coin is that highly efficient national administrations – such as the British – are prone to over-implement. Via a process known as 'gold plating', they implement more stringent regulations than have been agreed upon (increasing the proclivity of their businesses to complain about over-regulation by 'Brussels').

The sheer scope and complexity of European integration make it a nightmare for national administrations. New member states in particular face a steep learning curve. Possibly the most effective way to learn is through holding the Presidency of the Council, which rotates between the member states on a six-monthly basis. Certainly, the system, which came under sustained attack during the Convention on the Future of Europe, causes problems. For one thing, it is hardly a recipe for constancy. In the realm of foreign policy it is noticeable how different Presidencies usher in different priorities, with the Finns introducing a Northern Dimension, the Spanish and French focusing on a southern strategy and so on. None of the Union's neighbours thus feels ignored for too long, but this is presumably not the point. Yet there are advantages to a system that plays a crucial role in 'Europeanizing' national administrations. The post holder is responsible for arranging and chairing all Council meetings, setting agendas, and carrying out informal conversations with other member states about all manner of ongoing negotiations. Once an administration has experienced the Presidency, it understands the EU.

Administration and politics, of course, interact.

Governments with effective bureaucracies know that anything they sign up to in Brussels will be turned into law at home. For them, therefore, caution may be the order of the day when it comes to negotiating in Brussels (and states, it should be remembered, negotiate *in* and not *with* 'Brussels').

How states negotiate may also be a function of the way they decide on their negotiating strategy. Commission proposals can affect several national ministries in different ways. Take car emissions. Ministries of industry, health, environment and transport would all want a say in defining a national position on Commission legislative proposals in this area. And, given the nature of Council 'silos', who gets to negotiate what can be crucial. Some member states, notably France and Britain, coordinate the positions of their various ministries carefully and precisely. Their negotiators in the Council therefore often have very clear 'red lines' limiting the concessions they can make without overstepping their mandate. Other member states do things differently. In the good old days, the Federal Republic of Germany did not generally kick up much of a fuss about anything in the Council. Belgium occasionally kicks up even less of one: Belgian law insists that agreement must be reached between the various regional authorities before the Belgian negotiator can actually speak in the Council. Each approach has its merits. In combination they determine how effectively the Union functions. If everyone negotiated as the Belgians do, the Council would, on occasion, be a blissfully quiet place. If everyone were British or French, the system would grind to a halt.

Finally, it is worth bearing in mind that European integration fosters divisions *within* every bit as much as it can
between member states. One of the reasons why national
parliamentarians can be so acerbic in their criticisms of the
Union's supposed 'democratic deficit' (see chapter 7) is that
their governments on occasion use the EU as a means of
escaping from their clutches. While Danish parliamentarians have developed highly effective methods of scrutinizing
what their government agrees to in Brussels, others are less
effective. The German government, for instance, has
strongly resisted pressure from the Bundestag for a parliamentary vote on enlargements. The German government of
the early 1990s, fearful of a wave of immigrants crossing
from the newly liberated East, deliberately pressed for an
EU solution to the problem, conscious as it was of the constitutional hurdles it would have to cross (involving a need
for large parliamentary majorities) to alter its own asylum
provisions.

★

Several things can be said about the way the EU works.
Perhaps most importantly, it is the epitome of a consensus-
based system. For all the rhetoric one hears about Brussels
'imposing' regulations on member states, nothing could be
further from the truth. In fact the EU system makes contested decisions almost impossible to take. As one former
senior Commission official put it: 'Being based on dialogue,
the Community bears little resemblance to the concept of

government in the traditional sense of the word. The Community does not have a single head or a single leader. Decisions are collective and taken only after much confrontation of viewpoints.'[25] This is clearly the case in the intergovernmental pillars, which function by unanimity. In the first pillar too, however, negotiation is the order of the day. In both the Council and the European Parliament, the majorities needed to legislate are large and hard to assemble (particularly, in the case of the Parliament, because of absenteeism, which means a majority can equate to two thirds of those present).[26] And, of course, the Council does not always choose to use majority voting even in circumstances where the treaties would permit it to do so.

It is an ingenious system, and a delicate one. The phrase 'institutional balance' has been coined to emphasize this fragility, and the fact that empowering one part of the system at the expense of others risks undermining the delicate balancing act between national and European concerns. Increasingly, however, it is a system under strain. Tensions between the large and small member states have become increasingly acerbic in recent years, and it is no coincidence that the declaration to mark the fiftieth anniversary of the Treaty of Rome stated that the EU is based 'on equal rights'. Strains also emanate from the fact that even this consensus-based system has come under threat from member states anxious to preserve their independence.

At the beginning of the 1990s, a respected Brussels-based commentator observed that 'The Community Method has... now established itself so strongly that it is difficult to believe that efforts to halt, let alone reverse, the process of assimilation... will be very successful.'[27] Pressures on the Commission, the introduction of new decision-making processes and increasing member state wariness in general call this statement into doubt. The question now is to what extent this unique system still manages to work in practice.

4

MAKING THE MARKET

Y ou don't,' commented Jacques Delors in 1994, 'fall
in love with a common market.' He had a point.
Adoration is, frankly, an unrealistic expectation. So
too, it would appear, is simple appreciation. Francis
Fukuyama, in his widely celebrated article proclaiming the
'end of history', poured scorn upon 'those flabby, prosper-
ous, self-satisfied, inward-looking weak-willed states whose
grandest project was nothing more heroic than the creation
of the Common Market.'[1] The former French Prime
Minister Édouard Balladur was equally scathing, if less eloquent, about a world 'in which Europe was a trading area, a
large market, a Customs Union, without any strong con-
tents on decisions'.[2]

Such opinions, albeit widespread, are ill judged and ill
informed. Partly, incomprehension stems from the conditions under which the single market was conceived. Its
genesis lay in the need for a response to the economic crisis
of the 1970s and early 1980s. And, as we saw in chapter 2,
ambiguity concerning its ultimate nature was a necessary

precondition for agreement between political leaders with vastly different conceptions as to the desirable relationship between states and markets. Consequently the single market was sold by political leaders to their populations as a technical, apolitical undertaking that would painlessly serve to improve Europe's economic performance.

Little wonder, then, that it is so often taken for granted. Yet not only has the single market been the basis of many of the other successes achieved by European integration, but, in and of itself, it represents a considerable achievement. Combining a collection of national mixed economies into a transnational single market is an intensely political undertaking. While agreement on the need to remove barriers was relatively easy to arrive at, consensus over how this would occur, whether these barriers would be replaced by common standards or not, and how far EU competence should extend were deliberately left as matters for further negotiation. These negotiations are, to a significant extent, occurring only now.

★

It is hard to overstate the significance of the single market. The IMF, in its April 2007 World Ecnomic Outlook Database, reported that EU GDP was higher than that of the United States (£15.8 trillion versus £11.6 trillion). The impact of the single market project itself, of course, is harder to pin down, in that attempting to do so involves a tricky counterfactual concerning what would have happened in its absence. The Commission attempted such an undertaking as part of its campaign to sell the notion, commissioning a report which estimated the costs of maintaining barriers between national economies. Its 'findings' (economists tend to use this word when 'best guess' would perhaps be more apposite) was that business stood to save some €8 billion, and governments €1 billion if just frontier controls were abolished. More broadly, it projected an increase in EU GDP of 4.5–4.8 per cent.[3]

A follow-up study by the Commission itself was more measured, arguing that the single market had added a little over 1 per cent to EU GDP. Yet it went on to point out (and it's something too easily overlooked by politicians and commentators alike) that one reason for the relatively low figure was an unfavourable microeconomic policy environment attributable, in part at least, to the massive economic implications of German unification.[4] Nevertheless, in reflecting on ten years since the launch of the single market, the Commission was bullish in its claims, asserting that EU GDP was 1.8 per cent higher because of it, around 2.5 million jobs had been created that would not otherwise have existed, and a large increase in exports to third countries could be attributed to it. This was in addition to wider choice for consumers, lower tariffs – particularly in aviation and telecommunications – and, since 1993, a growth in intra-EU trade that outstripped that of GDP, so binding the EU economies still closer together.[5]

The sheer size of the single market implies that, however apparently trivial the individual measures necessary to

achieve it, their impact is considerable. Take chocolate. In
the late 1990s, the Union began discussions on a chocolate
directive. Media reaction was predictable enough, as negotiators bickered over vegetable fat, cocoa butter and milk
content. Yet chocolate is big business. Big both in countries
like Britain, where cocoa content is not considered a matter
of concern, and in Belgium, where the notion that chocolate be made out of milk and vegetable fat is heretical. A
directive regulating permissible quantities of these ingredi-
ents would clearly have massive implications Nor were
these limited to Europe. Some 90 per cent of the cocoa
beans used in European chocolate are imported from West
Africa. On the continent as a whole, 1.2 million cocoa producers, and some 11 million people, depend on cocoa for a
living. Some estimates had it that the directive agreed on
would cut African producers' revenues by around $800
million. Technical and apparently tedious it might be, but
the market matters.

★

The most bitter debates about the single market have concerned the degree to which it is an exercise simply in
reducing regulation (deregulation).[6] Fears that the single
market involves nothing but the removal of hard-won social
and health and safety benefits has increasingly come to
underpin scepticism about the EU in countries like France.
The argument deployed by many is that the principle of
mutual recognition, enshrined in the Cassis ruling, implies a

'competition among rules'. Governments find themselves unable to exclude goods manufactured in other member states, even if, by virtue of the lower social or health and safety provisions in those countries, these goods undercut those sold by domestic producers. The outcome is a 'race to the bottom', in which governments compete to create the most deregulated environment for business.

The reality is far more complex. First and foremost, it helps to be clear about terminology. Deregulation and re-regulation can be taken to have both quantitative and qualitative connotations. In the former sense, replacing twenty-seven national regulations with one European rule is deregulatory. Yet, qualitatively, this makes little sense if the one is significantly more onerous than any of those it replaces.

In the early years of the EEC, as we've seen, the Commission viewed harmonization as the logical instrument by which to drive market creation forward. National rules would thus be replaced by EC legislation. Yet the need for consensus in the Council meant that new regulations frequently required years of painful negotiation and even then were sometimes not approved. The Cassis ruling opened up new possibilities in the form of mutual recognition, severely limiting the right of member states to prevent the sale on their territory of any product lawfully produced or marketed in another. Mutual recognition removed the need for time-consuming legislation, with harmonization limited to minimum essential requirements.

Yet this was hardly unproblematic. A 1999 Commission

study indicated that mutual recognition is most effective when relatively simple products are involved and far less successful when they are complex.[7] Mutual recognition can also breed uncertainty regarding the extent to which products from one member state can enter the market of another without modification – it implies knowledge of the various regulatory systems in place. The Commission estimated that a failure to apply the principle of mutual recognition properly cut the trade in goods within the single market by up to 10 per cent or €150 billion in 2000.[8]

Mutual recognition, in other words, is far from a panacea. Nor does its existence necessarily imply, as many proponents of the 'race to the bottom' thesis have claimed, the gradual erosion of regulatory safety nets, as states compete to provide the least regulated market. When mutual recognition is invoked, governments can still enforce national rules for a number of reasons, including public morality and public health and safety. If just cause can be shown by a member state, its partners face a stark choice. They can either forego market access, or seek to negotiate a compromise, harmonized regulation. Harmonization may be time-consuming, but if a producer finds their products excluded from a member state under mutual recognition, it may represent the only alternative.[9]

Community-level action to replace national rules also occurs because of shifts in public and political attitudes towards the very notion of regulation. National regulatory failures (including BSE in the UK and a scandal over contaminated blood in France), along with mounting public concern over new technologies (most notably GMOs), have fostered increasing reliance on the so-called 'precautionary principle' as a basis for intervention in the market by public authorities. This lowers the bar for regulation, allowing public authorities to intervene even in the absence of firm scientific data about risk levels.[10]

The deregulatory implications of the single market have also been limited by the process via which regulations are promulgated at the European level. The Commission has long championed environmental and consumer protection issues and these concerns are often reflected in its draft legislative proposals. The increasing legislative powers of the European Parliament, moreover, have allowed it to help shape these regulations. And, again, it has not proved reluctant to do so, with a notable example in 1989 when it successfully threatened a veto unless a directive limiting the exhaust emissions of small cars was strengthened (see the discussion of environmental policy, below).

Finally, although regulatory activity has come under fire as part of the drive for 'better regulation' discussed in the previous chapter, the results of this have been mixed at best. Industry Commissioner Günter Verheugen claimed in October 2006 that cutting 'red tape' could save around 25 per cent of administrative costs over five years, resulting in a net economic benefit of some €150 billion. The cost to business of compliance with EU regulation, he claimed, was some €600 billion annually. Yet, while quick to condemn regulations with which they disagree, member states are equally anxious to protect those that benefit them. Thus, in

debates on the need to simplify complex rules spelling out
the packaging requirements for around seventy consumer
products, furious lobbying from certain member states
ensured that national rules on package sizes for butter, dried
pasta, coffee and white sugar will remain in place. Once
again, member states seem all too willing to tolerate a disjuncture between their rhetoric and their actions.

Particularly in the environmental and consumer protection fields, the EU has proved willing to replace national
regulations with harmonized European ones. The situation
as regards social policy, however, has been far different. EU
competence in the social sphere is modest at best, with core
aspects of social policy remaining national concerns. Thus,
social security questions related to employment contracts,
worker representation and employment policy funding are
subject to unanimity in the Council. Issues relating to pay,
the right of association and the right to strike are explicitly
excluded from the Union's remit.[11]

Consequently, many EU 'social policies' are little more
than declaratory initiatives intended to belie the impression
of market creation as a neoliberal, deregulatory affair. The
1989 Community Charter of the Fundamental Social Rights
of Workers argued that 'the completion of the single market
must lead to an improvement in the living and working conditions of workers' but itself changed nothing; a largely
ineffective European Employment Strategy was devised to
complement the Stability and Growth Pact; and the –
revealingly little-known – second clause of the 'Lisbon declaration' spoke of the need for 'more and better jobs and

greater social cohesion'. Rhetoric without substance has served merely to raise expectations which the Union has no means of matching.

Actual social policy activity has been largely limited to two areas. First, health and safety. As pointed out in chapter 2, working conditions were made subject to majority vote in the Council as a sop to those concerned by the deregulatory bias of the single market project. The implications have been far-reaching, particularly in the form of the 1993 Working Time Directive, stipulating minimum provisions for rest periods, shift work, night work, and health and safety protection, of which more below.

Second, in the absence of specific social legislation, the Court has made use of provisions in the treaty guaranteeing basic rights to promote social rights. Thus, under the principle of equality enshrined in the treaty, the ECJ insisted on equal retirement ages (with the significant cost implications this entailed for member state governments). And when, in 1990, it issued a similar ruling concerning occupational pensions (the Barber case), the member states were moved to append the so-called Barber Protocol to the Maastricht Treaty, which insisted on the non-retroactive nature of the ruling.[12] With the Amsterdam and Nice treaties including provisions against discrimination on the grounds of race, religion, disability, age or sexual orientation, we can expect to see more court activity in the years to come.

★

Enshrined in the logic of the single market programme was a belief that competition represents the most effective way of making economies function efficiently. Yet governments and firms do not always act accordingly, and can be remarkably creative when it comes to attempting to circumvent these provisions. Herein lies the basis of a clash between the EU and its member states.

Most economists hold that competition leads to greater diversification of products, rapid innovation and lower prices for consumers. The 'survival of the fittest' behaviour it encourages, in other words, brings economic benefits. Clearly this may not always be the case. There is scope for legitimate debate as to whether competition should be encouraged in all sectors and at all times. Not all member states, as we shall see, believe in free and open competition in sensitive sectors like energy. And President Sarkozy of France insisted upon the removal of 'undistorted competition' from the Union's objectives in negotiations over the Lisbon Treaty.

Yet all the member states have signed up to a treaty which guarantees competition in the single market if not as an overall objective of the EU. The problem is that such competition does not simply occur naturally. Without enforcement, firms may indulge in uncompetitive activities such as creating monopolies or cartels in order to keep prices artificially high and restrict consumer choice. Governments, too, may distort competition by providing benefits (state aids) to certain firms (be it in the form of cash or 'in kind' support such as new road or rail links), thereby reducing their need to compete as hard with their rivals. Competition, as Peter Sutherland, a former Commissioner for Competition (1985–9), and avid rugby fan put it, is 'a level playing field where individual talent, effort and comparative advantage lead to victory, rather than an inclined pitch with moving goalposts, a biased referee and an opposing team full of steroids'.[13]

In the EU, as we have seen, it is the Commission that is the referee, wielding the power to police antitrust policy, mergers and state aids. And it has proved more than willing to deploy these powers. High-profile decisions have included that to make the French utilities giant Électricité de France repay €900 million of illegal aid to the French government. Even more striking was the decision, confirmed in September 2007, to fine Microsoft the sum of €497 million while obliging it to share information on its Windows system with its rivals. The number of 'dawn raids' on firms to seize documents related to possible unfair practices has increased substantially (from four in 1996 to twenty-one in 2003). In 2006, the Commission carried out simultaneous raids on twenty sites belonging to the biggest European energy firms amid allegations that they had restricted access to pipeline and storage facilities. And as investigations have increased in number, so, too, have the fines levied. While the total in the 1990s amounted to €946 million, fines of €3,080 million were imposed between 2000 and 2003.[14] And new rules introduced in 2006 mean that penalties could be imposed on companies to the equivalent of 10 per cent of their annual turnover, and proportional to the duration of the abuse. In a sign of things to come, in February 2007 the Commission imposed a record €992 million fine on ThyssenKrupp and four other lift manufacturers.

So successful has the Commission proven in pursuing cartels that its Directorate General for Competition was, in 2006, named the most admired antitrust agency in the world. *Global Competition Review*, in its annual ranking of antitrust agencies (based on responses from national competition authorities and interviews with lawyers, executives and economists) found that recent 'improvements are starting to bed down and [the Commission's] responsiveness should be praised. It is willing to take on difficult cases and is getting impressive cartel results. DG Comp is the agency most admired by other enforcers.'

Yet such eulogies hide profound difficulties. While the Commission has investigated several high-profile mergers with the potential to distort competition, its competence is limited to those above a certain threshold. For instance, if both companies have more than two thirds of their turnover within a member state, it is for authorities in that member state to decide. Hence the Commission was forced to conclude that it did not have authority to rule on the proposed merger between Spanish firms Endesa and Gas Naturel in 2005, or on that between Suez and Gaz de France, both of which had enormous implications in terms of the development of an EU energy market – not least as national regulators cannot always be relied upon to be immune from political influence (see below).

Perhaps the most sensitive aspect of the Commission's remit is its role in policing the part played by governments in undermining competition. State aid policy involves direct confrontations between member state governments – who provide the aid in the first place – and the European Commission. Clearly, a single market could be undermined if member states can effectively protect their industries by providing them with state funds. Yet preventing this involves a unique undertaking of enormous proportions. Simply put, the Commission is tasked by the treaties to tell national governments what they can and cannot spend their money on within their own borders. It has done so with some success. In 1988, state aid accounted for 10 per cent of public expenditure, or 3–5 per cent of GDP. By 2002, those figures had fallen to about 1.2 per cent of public expenditure and 0.6 per cent of GDP.[15] Yet member states are still willing to use public funds to subsidize economic activity. Some €53 billion was provided in 2003, with Germany, France and Italy being the chief culprits. The December 2005 state aid scorecard found that €61.6 billion had been spent in 2004. Constant vigilance (as J. K. Rowling's Mad Eye Moody might put it) is necessary, therefore, to ensure that such public financing does not erode competition.

In such a complex and technical field, where the Commission is responsible for policing not only the European market but also the actions of member states all too adept at dissimulation, resources are vital. And they are lacking. DG Competition has a staff of only some 700, with a mere 300 senior officials. As Stephen Wilks has put it, the 'only plausible explanation for under-resourcing is that member states see resources as one of the few pragmatic ways in which to restrain the ambitions of the DG'.[16] Little surprise, then, that investigations into complex competition cases take time, with that culminating in the 2004 fine against Microsoft having been launched in 1999. Nor that member states are reluctant to provide increased funds to enable more effective scrutiny of their own actions. While accepting the need for EU action in numerous domains, governments remain unwilling to allow its institutions the resources necessary to enforce these against national capitals (i.e. against themselves).

★

A 2005 Commission report states baldly that 'Internal Market integration is stagnating', pointing to the absence of price convergence and the slowing of trade between member states.[17] The market is also, moreover, characterized by a striking 'home bias'. For all the talk of a single European economic space, Europeans still tend to shop and invest predominantly in their own countries. The population of the EU15 spend 86 per cent of their expenditure on national products, 10 per cent on products from rest of the EU and 4 per cent from other OECD countries. An average EU15 member state invests 65 per cent of its equity wealth at home and 18 per cent in other EU15 countries.[18]

The market is also somewhat patchy, with some sectors lagging behind others. Thus, there is significantly less cross-border merger and acquisition activity in the financial services sector than in others. The Commission has expressed particular concern about the continued fragmentation of retail financial services markets, which in turn will have an impact on the performance of the euro.[19] The lack of progress is partly due to the difficult balancing act involved in reconciling the opposition of some – notably many London-based financial institutions – to new rules with a desire to harmonize regulations in the market.

Even in those areas where legislative initiatives have proven possible, numerous reports reveal persistent failures on the part of member states to implement these laws correctly. A report of January 2005 revealed that more than a quarter of the rules governing the single market were not put into effect in at least one country. The number of open infringement cases had risen from just under 700 in 1992 to just over 1,500 by 2002.[20]

Since 1997, as we have seen, the Commission has published regular internal market 'scorecards' naming and shaming the worst offenders in terms of the transposition of directives. The so-called 'transposition deficit' represents the percentage of internal market directives not yet communicated as having been fully transposed as a proportion of the total number of directives which should have been. In November 2004, it stood at 3.6 per cent (2.9 per cent for the EU15) – a significant increase on previous years. The Commission was still waiting for 1,428 notifications of transposition from the member states, and 27 per cent of legislation had not been fully transposed in at least one

member state; several of the older member states –
Belgium, Luxembourg, Italy and Greece – recorded their
worst transposition deficit for years in 2004.[21] Figures
released in February 2007 revealed something of an
improvement, though only time will tell if this represents
anything more than a blip. The fact remains that the achievement of a single market still depends on the willingness of
the member states to respect the obligations they have
made. Talking about a market is one thing. Creating one
requires firm action by national governments.

★

Three recent areas of Union activity – debates over the liberalization of services, plans for an EU energy policy and
environmental policy – serve to illustrate in more tangible
form the kinds of problems increasingly confronting efforts
at market creation.

Although explicitly covered under the freedoms enunci-
ated in the Treaty of Rome, a number of barriers prevent
the provision of services across borders within the Union.[22]
Commission figures estimate that services make up some 70
per cent of the EU economy. In 2005, 116 million people
were employed in the sector. Foreign investment between
the EU15 was eight times higher for services than for manufacturing in 2000.[23]

Yet the bewildering variety of barriers restricting cross-
border trade in services means that this accounts for only 20
per cent of intra-EU trade. Many see this lack of competition

as responsible for a lack of competitiveness. Productivity growth in the sector has, on average, been less than 0.5 per cent in the eurozone as compared to 3 per cent in the US.[24] Services are big business, and a single market that does not incorporate them is a single market in name only.

Admittedly such figures, while striking, are somewhat overstated. After all, many services providers – hairdressers, for example – would not trade across borders even if doing so were made easier. Thus, simply to assume potential benefits from the size of the sector may be misleading. Yet the services sector is, undeniably, riddled with often ridiculous restrictions on foreign providers, be they French stipulations that service workers from another member state have to register eight days prior to carrying out a repair, or the need for tour guides in some member states to have licences, or regulations specifying the minimum distance between opticians (though a strong case can be made for similar legislation covering mobile phone shops).

There are, in other words, powerful incentives for some kind of liberalization. And this is precisely what the Commission proposed on 13 January 2004, when it presented draft legislation designed to create an internal market in services, thereafter known as the 'Bolkestein directive' (after the Internal Market Commissioner, Frits Bolkestein). Two principles lay at the directive's heart. The first was freedom of establishment. The often cumbersome process of setting up in another member state would be simplified through provision of 'one-stop shops' in each member state to authorize and register foreign service providers. Second, and far more controversially, service delivery would be governed by the 'country of origin' principle. Providers would, initially, be subject to the laws of their country of origin rather than of the country where the service was being delivered. Thus, they could test a new market – a step that often foreshadows establishment – without undertaking the potentially expensive process of complying with all its regulations.

The text proved highly controversial. Of the member states, Belgium, France, Germany and Italy voiced particularly strong opposition. In March 2005, 100,000 marched through the streets of Brussels in protest against the draft legislation. Jacques Chirac deemed the proposal unacceptable, while others branded it the 'Frankenstein directive'. Politics took over and, as ever, organized and well-funded producer interests proved far more vocal and effective lobbyists than the consumers who stood to benefit from liberalization and lower prices. As a consequence, the European Parliament insisted on a significant watering down of the draft, to such an extent that its heart – the country of origin principle – was torn out and a number of sectors included within the original draft (such as social services, health care and public transport) were removed.

There is a real danger that, rather than simplifying cross-border service provision, the compromise legislation eventually agreed upon will merely complicate things still further. Service providers will need to be *au fait* not only with the treaty and sector-specific services legislation, but also the services directive itself in order to ascertain their rights with regard to delivery and establishment. And this is particularly problematic in a sector disproportionately made up of small and medium-sized enterprises which cannot afford the costs – in either time or legal expenses – of ensuring compliance with a myriad different rules and regulations. Only time will tell, moreover, whether differential administrative systems in the member states will imply a proliferation of vastly different forms of one-stop shop for those wishing to establish in another member state.

'Fear,' declared the Commission's President Barroso, 'is something which sells better than hope.' He was right. Opponents of the legislation fought a campaign based on fears, many of them misplaced (the Polish plumber, emblematic of French concerns about an influx of cheap labour from Central and Eastern Europe, being the most obvious case in point, there being only some fifty of them in the whole of France in 2005). Yet the Commission, equally, should know better than to legislate on the basis of hope. The original text left much room for ambiguity – one French wag wondered whether the country of origin principle meant a British plumber working in Paris would be allowed to drive to the job on the left. Moreover, the details of what length of stay constituted establishment as opposed to delivery remained vague at best (leaving open the question as to how long a provider could operate under home country rules). Admittedly, there was good reason for this – tennis coaches require different arrangements to plumbers.

But leaving such things to future litigation was hardly a way of reassuring those anxious about the potential effects of liberalization, particularly given the all-encompassing scope of the original draft.

The services debacle illustrated three fundamental aspects of the contemporary Union. First, the prominence that debates over the single market have now achieved, in stark contrast to the profound lack of public interest that greeted the White Paper which launched it some two decades previously. High-profile political interventions, large-scale demonstrations and aggressive lobbying all served to underline the degree to which the market has become politically salient.

Moreover, the tone of the debate reflected increasing uncertainties in some member states about the very project of market creation. Partly, this was due to timing. The unveiling of the directive coincided with eastward enlargement and the influx of significant numbers of East Europeans into Germany in particular. Partly, too, opponents of the directive reflected a growing sense that, far from representing a defence against globalization, European integration was becoming synonymous with it, exposing particularly the richer West European economies to unfair (that is to say, cheaper) competition from the new member states. Again, such fears were largely unfounded and reflected more the willingness of opponents of the directive to use any arguments that suited them than anything to do with reality.[25] Yet they are proving increasingly influential in shaping attitudes towards the market.

Finally, we come again to the issue of trust. To accept the country of origin principle, the host country must have a significant degree of trust in the standards and safeguards in place in the home state. Yet this is in increasingly short supply in a larger, more heterogeneous and more intrusive Union. And the erosion of trust represents a challenge not only to the mutual recognition principle at the heart of the single market undertaking. More broadly, such suspicions represent a challenge to the integration process as a whole. As chapter 3 made clear, the Union is a system that functions on the basis of consensus and voluntary compliance more than on majoritarianism and coercion. In a climate of distrust, that system will come under severe strain.

Energy is another issue that continues to dominate the EU agenda. The origins of European integration lay in energy. The Coal and Steel Community set the scene, followed by EURATOM, whose creation accompanied that of the EEC. EEC leaders spoke periodically in terms of the development of a genuine EU energy policy. The 1972 Paris summit communiqué requested that 'the Community institutions... formulate as soon as possible an energy policy guaranteeing certain and lasting supplies under satisfactory economic conditions'.

Nothing came of such initiatives. Yet, some fifty years after its first forays into the energy field, European integration again began to concern itself with the sector, with a series of directives aimed at the completion of a single energy market. In 1996 and 1998, the first electricity and gas directives were passed, with the aim of allowing industrial consumers to choose their energy suppliers freely by July 2004 (with householders being in a position to do the same by July 2007). The directives were merely the opening salvo of a struggle that continues to this day.

Two developments in particular have conspired to give energy particular prominence over the last couple of years. First, and most importantly, the issue of security of energy supplies has shot up the political agenda. The proximate cause has been the behaviour of Russia, which, in January 2006 and again the following year, cut gas deliveries as part of 'negotiations' with its neighbours over energy prices. In the former instance, gas supplies to France fell by 30 per cent, with even bigger declines being registered in Central and Eastern Europe.

Subsequently, European political leaders began to fret about their energy dependence. The Commission's paper on energy, released in January 2007, argued that energy import dependence was set to rise from 50 per cent of total consumption to 65 per cent in 2030. For gas, the figures were from 57 per cent to 84 per cent, for oil a staggering increase from 82 per cent to 93 per cent.[26] As one Slovakian diplomat put it in early 2006, even 'culture ministers have energy issues on the agendas for meetings'. The G8 issued a joint statement on global energy security, reflecting concern about their increased dependence for oil and gas on politically or economically insecure regions such as the Middle East and Russia.

Security of supply considerations combined with a host of other factors in creating conditions conducive to the development of an ambitious new energy policy initiative. These factors included concerns engendered by the black-outs that hit much of continental Europe in November 2006 (caused by an overloading of electricity lines in northern Germany), affecting millions in Germany, France, Italy and Spain; a desire to cut greenhouse gas emissions; and a belief that the creation of a single energy market would be economically more efficient, leading to increasing trade and lower prices.

Yet it soon became clear that the original energy directives had failed to make much of an impact. In November 2005, the preliminary findings of a Commission competition enquiry emphasized the problem of market concentration. On the one hand, the original legislation had proved relatively successful in promoting liberalization, notably through the privatization of state-owned energy companies (such as Electrabel in Belgium). Yet not only do many of the largest players remain in state hands, but, although there was a significant increase in cross-border mergers — the Commission spoke of a 75 per cent rise between 2000 and 2005 — the new private firms still for the most part enjoyed monopoly positions, and energy supply remained stubbornly national. The electricity market was in reality a string of national grids with few bilateral links — the Spanish market is almost entirely self-contained; less then 10 per cent of European gas is sold across borders.[27]

Liberalization in fact heralded a rush for national consolidation. In late 2005, the German government ignored the arguments of the its Cartel Office and Monopolies

Commission, allowing E.ON to merge with Ruhrgas, Germany's biggest gas company. In France, the proposed €70 billion merger of Suez and Gaz de France was orchestrated largely in order to prevent a takeover of the former by the Italian energy firm Enel. The political motives for the manoeuvre were clearly discernible in the disappointed reaction of Suez shareholders at what they saw as the blatant undervaluation of the company – some estimated by as much as a third.

Anti-competitive practices are connived at and even encouraged by governments anxious to maintain the positions of their national energy champions. Following a bid from the Germany energy giant E.ON for the Spanish firm Endesa in February 2006, the government in Madrid passed legislation extending the powers of its energy regulator. Henceforth, it would be allowed to block foreign takeovers on a number of spectacularly vague grounds, including 'protection of the general interest and reasons of public security'. Certainly, this will allow it to block takeovers by non-EU firms. It also, however, has the effect of inhibiting the creation of a genuine EU energy market. The bottom line was that the government favoured a lower bid for Endesa from a Spanish group.

In the face of such challenges, the Commission has redoubled its efforts to force open the market. In March 2005, it referred Belgium, Greece, Latvia, Luxembourg and Spain to the ECJ for failing to transpose the electricity directive. A year later, buoyed by the apparent success of the draft Energy Policy it had presented to the March 2006

European Council, it threatened legal action against seventeen member states for failing to open their markets.

The Commission targeted three issues in particular. First, collusion or cartel activity between larger firms, which served to restrict the access of potential competitors to their markets. Second, the use of long-term – as long as fifteen years – supply contracts to tie consumers in to deals with suppliers (the German cartel office is engaged in an ongoing argument with E.ON about long-term contracts on the grounds that these are unfair to newcomers seeking market access). Finally, what has come to be known as 'unbundling', or the need to bring to an end a situation in which energy infrastructure is in the hands of incumbent supply companies, providing them with multiple opportunities to discriminate against competing suppliers. The 'bundling' of infrastructure and supply services also means that companies have little incentive to invest in infrastructure for the creation of a genuine European network – infrastructure that would permit foreign competitors to intrude on their territory.

Member states have remained divided. Debates over unbundling represent a good example. The row pitted the UK, Ireland, the Netherlands, Denmark, Finland, Belgium, Portugal, Hungary and Romania against France, Poland, Spain and Slovakia. The former, more liberally minded group, accept Commission arguments about the need to prevent the same companies being in charge of both infrastructure and supply. The latter, in contrast, believe in the effectiveness of managed national markets dominated by quasi-monopolistic companies, arguing that this represents the optimal method of guaranteeing security of supply. The French government, in its official response to the Commission's March 2006 Green Paper, argued that unbundling would dilute investment capacities and be detrimental both to security of supply and to consumers, who benefited from regulated energy prices.

In 2006, the Commission had called vociferously for full unbundling. Yet stubborn opposition – from France and Germany in particular – led to Barroso conceding that this was not politically possible.[28] Commission proposals of January 2007 represented a fudge, providing for two options: on the one hand, full unbundling; on the other, the so-called Independent System Operator scheme (ISO). Under this, integrated companies continue to own but are not responsible for the operation, maintenance or development of network assets from which they will continue to receive revenue. It seems likely that the latter option will be adopted. It is messy, and will provide fewer incentives for investment in transnational infrastructure, and any such decisions taken by the Independent Systems Operators will be strongly contested. The ISO scheme, moreover, will require detailed regulation for what is an enormously complex economic sector in order to ensure that control, as opposed to ownership, is in properly independent hands. It is surely only a matter of time before the Commission finds itself on the receiving end of abuse for imposing excessively bureaucratic regulations, while certain member states, no doubt, do their utmost to avoid their obligations.

More broadly, the Union's energy strategy is hamstrung by its partial competence over the sector. Alongside highly upbeat declarations about the birth of an energy policy for Europe have come repeated reminders that the member states have their own rights. The much-heralded March 2006 European Council declaration on energy asserts baldly that the Energy Policy for Europe should 'fully respect member states' sovereignty over primary energy sources and choice of energy mix'. Yet it is hard to see how the Union can adequately address the issues of security of supply or, particularly, the reduction of greenhouse emissions that were emphasized in the Commission's 2007 paper while member states remain in charge of the choice of energy sources. How can emissions be addressed if nuclear power remains off the agenda? How can security of supply be monitored at the European level if member states are free to make their own arrangements when it comes to securing energy? As if to make the point, just over a month after the Energy Policy for Europe was signed, and with no prior discussion with its partners, Germany signed its own arrangements for a €5 billion gas pipeline with Russia. The Polish Defence Minister likened the deal (the pipeline would run under the Baltic, circumventing Poland and Belarus) to the 1939 Molotov–Ribbentrop pact.

The very fact that the Commission has seen fit to issue highly ambitious proposals bears eloquent testimony to the transborder nature of the energy sector. Shortages in one country have an impact on others, while the environmental consequences of energy consumption do not afflict merely the state where that consumption occurs. Yet transnational policy problems are not always amenable to easy transnational solutions. As pointed out in chapter 1, the mere existence of strong incentives for institutionalized cooperation do not guarantee that states will opt for such cooperation. Both the need for consensus and a lack of competence raise the spectre of EU policies achieving merely the worst of all worlds. Halfway between competence and spectator status, between liberalization and the continuation of monopolistic practices, its policy promises much but risks delivering far less.

Environmental policy is very different. It is one area where the Union has shown a particular proclivity to regulate the market. Its response to the environmental challenges confronting it represents one of the clearest examples of the benefits member states can derive from common action in an EU framework. Environmental problems are self-evidently trans-border in nature. Yet the cost of the measures necessary to confront them can be prohibitive. The existence of the single market, however, has two potentially positive effects. First, because member states acting through the Union all have to adopt the same regulations, they need not fear their closest trading partners gaining a comparative advantage as a consequence of their environmentalist initiatives. More broadly, and discussed in more length in the next chapter, the sheer size and international weight of the single market means that the Union's trading partners have an incentive to adopt equivalent standards in order to ensure access to it.

Consequently, the Union has become something of a world leader in the environmental sphere. Environmental concerns figure prominently among its stated objectives. The 1998 Cardiff summit introduced the (imaginatively named) 'Cardiff process', whereby environmental policy would be integrated into all aspects of EU policy, while Article 177 of the Amsterdam Treaty placed sustainable development at the heart of EU cooperation programmes with the outside world.

The Union has launched six environmental action programmes (the latest covering 2002–2012). Among its major initiatives have been the 1976 Bathing Water directive (updated in February 2006), limiting sewage discharge in proximity to bathing areas; the Habitats directive of 1992, establishing an EU network of nature conservation sites; the 1999 Landfill directive laying down common standards, and various pieces of legislation covering drinking water. Most recently, debates over the Registration, Evaluation and Authorization of Chemicals (REACH) directive revealed the willingness of the Union to take environmental considerations into account when legislating on the market. The directive required detailed information to be provided, and proper evaluation to be carried out on some 30,000 substances before they went on the market.

The focus of recent activity has, of course, been climate change. Indeed, remarkably, the first stated priority of the Commission's January 2007 communication on energy policy was the need to combat climate change. Never short of ambition, it called for a new global industrial revolution.[29]

The European Council of March that same year announced the imposition of dramatic, binding targets. These involved a minimum 20 per cent reduction of greenhouse gas emissions by 2020 (from 1990 levels), rising to 30 per cent if other developed countries committed themselves to similar reductions.[30]

A central plank of the Union's carbon reduction strategy has been the so-called Emission Trading Scheme (ETS). The ingenuity of this is the way it deploys market mechanisms to reduce greenhouse gas emissions. National allocation plans are produced for the number of carbon permits to be allowed for energy-intensive businesses such as electricity generation and steelmaking. Since 2005, around 12,000 large industrial plants, (estimated to cover some 40 per cent of EU CO_2 emissions) have been able to buy and sell permits to release CO_2. National Action Plans specifying emission levels for the period 2005–7 were submitted by the member states for approval by the Commission. Once agreed, fines of €40 per excess tonne emitted were imposed, with these set to rise to €100 under the second scheme, due to commence in 2008.

Well-meaning it certainly was, but the ETS was flawed in several respects. Member states, typically, managed to secure a whole raft of exemptions to the scheme, including the transport and building sectors (the largest polluters after power generation and energy-intensive industries). Moreover, individual plants could opt out, while 'flexibility' meant that circumstances such as cold weather could be considered as mitigating.

Yet the major problem has been the over-allocation of pollution credits. According to Commission figures published in May 2006, the problem was widespread: 1,785 billion tonnes were emitted in 2005, yet 1,829 billion tonnes' worth of permits had been issued. Germany, for instance, found itself left with 44.1 million tonnes of extra CO_2 allowances for 2005. Indeed, of all the large member states, only the UK emitted more than its quota, with British industries having to buy 30 million tonnes' worth of permits on the 'carbon market'.

The consequence of an over-allocation of permits, markets being markets, was a sharp fall in carbon prices to about €15 a tonne. And one does not need to be an economist to realize that if purchasing proves cheaper than fines (themselves set at a low level for the first period), the incentives for restraint were not great. Indeed, because a large proportion of the pollution permits were provided to businesses free of charge, several of the worst polluters contrived to receive windfall profits by selling their surplus credits.

Always anxious to make great play of their environmental ambitions, member states again, at the start of the second period of the ETS (2008–12), attempted to duck their commitments. By July 2006, only six of them had submitted definitive emissions plans to the Commission (the deadline for doing so was the end of June). Of the others, eight submitted drafts while the remaining thirteen had filed nothing whatsoever. By October, the Commission was considering legal action against nine who had still failed to submit their plans. Even those submitted were not always inspiring. A WWF spokesperson commented with regard to the Polish plan that the Commission should just 'send it back and say "rewrite"'.

In November 2006, the Commission published its appraisal of the eleven National Action Plans so far submitted for the next ETS period. And it rejected ten of the eleven (the UK being the exception) on the basis that their allocation of permits was, again, excessively generous. To take but one example, Lithuania had, for the period 2005–7, introduced a cap of 12.3 million tonnes; its 2005 emissions were 6.6 million. Nevertheless, just to be on the safe side the government proposed a cap for the 2008–12 period of 16.6 million. The Commission, for its part, insisted the figure be reduced to 8.8 million.

It should come as no surprise that member states did not react well to being lectured. Germany in early 2007 was said to be considering legal action after the Commission demanded a 6 per cent reduction in its proposed output (Berlin had first proposed 482 million tonnes and subsequently reduced this to 465; the Commission demanded 453.1). By January 2007, only the UK plan out of the ten so far evaluated fulfilled all the necessary criteria.

Clearly, member states had learnt from the Stability and Growth Pact. Better to fashion lax rules than risk opprobrium for breaking stringent ones. France was excluded from the list of sinners at the last moment, having withdrawn its plan (apparently to improve it). Again, it should come as no surprise that the French government placed

pressure on the Commission not to assess what had originally been submitted, leading the German Environment
Minister, Sigmar Gabriel, to comment that this was something 'we should talk about'.

Thus, behind the fine rhetoric, the Union faces severe
problems in adhering to the ambitious targets it sets itself.
This has also been apparent in attempts dramatically to
reduce car emissions (by something like a quarter of
current average levels). The Commission itself was profoundly divided on the issue. The Industry Commissioner,
Günter Verheugen, in a letter to Barroso, argued that 'our
environmental leadership could significantly undermine the
international competitiveness of part of Europe's energy-
intensive industries and worsen global environmental
performance by redirecting production to parts of the
world with lower environmental standards.'[31] At least envi-
ronmentalism has proceeded to such an extent that
opposition to it must now be couched in environmentalist
terms.

Verheugen (coincidentally, no doubt, a German Commissioner) was united in his anxieties with the German
government, which, although nominally impartial (because
holding the EU Presidency), lobbied furiously on behalf of
its car industry. That the likes of BMW and Mercedes were
vociferous opponents of plans their French and Italian counterparts increasingly came to support was a matter of
economics not ecological principle. Germans tend to make
big cars. Consequently stringent emissions limits would
place disproportionate burdens upon them. This approach

clearly infuriated the Commission, moving Barroso to declare to the magazine for German parliamentarians that the Commission could not 'simply tailor [its] criteria to the wishes of individual member states'.[32] But of course it could. Largely thanks to German lobbying, the Commission compromised on a target of 130g/km versus the 120g/km it had originally proposed.

As ever, and as the ETS illustrates all too clearly, implementation is a problem. Targets notwithstanding, the European Environment Agency reported in June 2006 that EU emissions of greenhouse gases increased by 0.4 per cent between 2003 and 2004. Figures for 2006 suggest an increase of between 1 and 1.5 per cent. And the even more ambitious targets set in March 2007 will depend on a successful outcome to difficult negotiations on how individual member states contribute to the overall target. Little surprise, then, that the Energy Commissioner, Andris Piebalgs, commented ruefully in September of that year that distributing environmental targets on green energy sources among twenty-seven states was proving to be 'quite a politically sensitive issue'. As with energy policy, moreover, a need to tiptoe round the nuclear issue left the environmental debates somewhat incomplete.

None of which should be taken to imply that the Union's environmental policies have been a failure. The EU has established itself as a world leader in the field. The very fact that member states such as Portugal, which had no environmental legislation on its statute books prior to accession, have signed up to the EU effort represents something of a triumph. Yet, equally, the Union should steer clear of what could turn into something of a Stalinist approach to target setting. Targets without delivery will be meaningless. And, as ever, delivery will depend on the member states respecting the rhetorical commitments they have made, and submitting to the requirements laid down for them by the Commission.

★

Above and beyond these very current challenges, the single market faces several further threats to its successful completion. For one thing, agreement over key pieces of single market legislation has proved elusive. A case in point was the EU Patents directive. Such a law would mean that a patent filed in one member state would be valid across the bloc. Under current arrangements, companies must translate them into different languages, fight infringements in several member state courts and pay twenty-five times to receive an EU-wide patent. Yet the legislation, deadlocked in Council for some twenty years, was rejected when revisited in December 2006.

Bad laws, moreover, can be equally counterproductive. A takeover directive was finally agreed in December 2003 – after fourteen years of negotiation. Yet the compromises necessary to achieve Council approval stripped the final text of much of its substance. Key articles preventing certain forms of defence against hostile takeovers without prior shareholder approval and limiting the legality of share and voting restrictions were made optional. Only the three Baltic states opted into the latter, while Germany, Denmark, Luxembourg, Poland and the Netherlands opted out of the former. A Commission report in February 2007 concluded sadly that the 'number of member states implementing the directive in a seemingly protectionist way is unexpectedly large'. Indeed, only five of them managed to get the law on their statute books at all before the deadline of May 2006.

The Commission's conclusions were totally in keeping with the proclivity of member states to contest even those provisions already enshrined in law. Whether it was the Polish government reacting angrily to Commission approval for a bank merger, or the explicit interference of the French and Spanish governments in attempted foreign takeovers of national energy giants, several member states seem to have forgotten their commitments to the construction of a European market. Indeed, French legislation drafted in 2005 and intended to make foreign takeovers of French firms more difficult seemed flatly to contradict such commitments.

There is a real danger, moreover, that such actions on the part of one member state have an effect on the attitudes of others. Romano Prodi, former Commission President and a man who really should have known better, was moved to declare that, if elected Prime Minister, he would block French companies from buying in Italy in retaliation for the failure on the part of Paris to open its own markets. And, indeed, a decree published in early April 2006 gave the

Italian government power of veto over takeovers of the country's largest gas distribution company, despite the known objections of the Commission. One East European official summed up the dangers when certain governments decided to pick and choose which obligations to respect: 'you don't let in the Polish plumber, you should not be surprised if we can't let in the Italian banker.'

Certainly, the Commission has reacted to signs of increasing member state intransigence. It announced in April 2006 that it would pursue infringement procedures against nineteen member states for their failure to implement one or more of eight different Internal Market Directives. Yet, again, the institution simply lacks the resources effectively to police a market of twenty-seven member states. And even if it could, the tendency of those same states to seek compromise in the Council rather than proceed by majority vote tends to produce vague, complex or simply badly drafted laws, endangering the Commission's ability to enforce them. Commissioners are increasingly left with recourse to forces much less stringent than law. In response to French plans to protect companies against hostile takeovers, the Internal Market Commissioner, Charlie McCreevy, was left to rue the fact that while 'these measures may be in line with the takeover directive, I believe they are contrary to the spirit of the movement of capital'. Franco Frattini, the Italian Commission Vice-President, similarly commented that the merger between Gaz de France and Suez may not have violated EU law, but was 'a blow to the spirit of the common European market'.

The willingness of member states to stymie the market is bad enough. Equally, if not more, troubling is the fact that their inability to agree on clear legislation leaves the way open for other institutions to act. Thus, the Court shocked member states when, in 2004, it decided that 'working time,' as specified under the 2003 directive, should include all the duty time of doctors, firemen and social workers, among others. The implications were huge. The British government estimated the cost of compliance (in that country alone) at £250 million. As UK minister Alistair Darling pointed out, the judgment was a 'clear warning to ministers that if they can't agree what they mean, or agree a compromise which is actually a fudge, the courts will step in and legislate for them at massive cost'. Forced to negotiate a new directive, the member states failed to reach agreement in 2006. Lack of consensus meant implementation of the original legislation. The Commission thus prepared to take legal action against all but Luxembourg and (unusually) Italy over their failure to implement the original draft.

Tax provides another salutary tale. Again, the Court has been instrumental. Two path-breaking judgments – on Marks and Spencer and Cadbury Schweppes – severely limited the right of the British government either to stop companies offsetting losses made by foreign companies against profits in the UK or taxing subsidiaries based elsewhere. The estimated cost of the latter decision alone was some £400 million annually.[33] The potential implications of the cases were thus huge. And, again, it was the absence of clear legislation or treaty stipulations on tax that left the way open for court action.

Health policy is another area of concern. So sensitive is it, in fact, that Germany, Spain, Belgium, Luxembourg, Portugal, Sweden, Italy and the UK have together created the Aachen Group in an attempt to protect national health systems. The EU formally has only a supporting role in the public health sphere. Yet the increasing prevalence of private health provision and of people willing to travel abroad to purchase it has altered the situation somewhat. A series of judgments in cases dating from the late 1990s have made it clear that the Court sees private provision of health care as an aspect of the single market. A recent case saw a UK citizen, Yvonne Watts, successfully claim that she was entitled to reimbursement from the NHS for treatment she had undergone in France because of the length of waiting times in the UK. That nine member states chose to be represented in proceedings served to illustrate its importance.

In the face of the Court's jurisprudence, member states face a dilemma. Under the terms of the treaty, they can either allow the ECJ to decide on the scope of EU social policy (even in face of their opposition) or encourage the Commission to come up with its own proposals – despite their opposition to an EU role in the sector. Hardly surprisingly the Commission, in 2006, announced its plans to table a directive on the opening up of the health services market.

Herein lies the real potential danger of market making. Because the social policies of the Union remain so limited, social welfare provision remains largely a national concern.

The legitimacy of such provision lies at the heart of what people like to refer to as the 'European social model'. In order to ensure a continued balance between market making at the European and social protection at the national levels, however, care must be taken to ensure that single market regulations do not provide a rationale for supranational meddling in national-level social policy provision (see the discussion on competence in chapter 7).

★

The single market is a massive undertaking that promises significant rewards while requiring, for its completion, substantial political effort. What the preceding discussion has illustrated is that it is up to the member states to ensure this completion. Partly, their recent hesitations can be put down to lack of interest. Politicians have a tendency to speak as if the market were complete, leaving them free to concentrate on newer, sexier, initiatives. As such, there are signs that the political will necessary to complete the market may be lacking.

Conversely, certain recent disputes have had the effect of challenging member state attachment to the market. John Monks, head of the European Trades Union Congress, observed that frantic lobbying in the Council over the new draft of the Working Time directive in 2006 represented the 'biggest diplomatic initiative seen in peacetime'.[34] No longer, then, can a market be made by stealth, and, indeed, without clear limits to its scope the member states face the prospect of supranational intrusion into ever more sensitive aspects of national life. These cannot but increase wariness about the project and the EU institutions championing it.

Yet these institutions, finally, are crucial. This chapter serves, if nothing else, to give the lie to those who assert the need for a market without the Union, arguing that the single market should be preserved, while the institutions of the EU are, at a minimum, reined in. This was one possible reading of Margaret Thatcher's Bruges speech. It is curious how, so often, those most in favour of the market are those who understand it the least. Without the Court and the Commission, there would be no single market. For all their stated commitments to it, the member states frequently baulk at the painful adjustments market creation implies for them. Certainly, their willingness to submit to supranational control has, to date, been remarkable when compared to the behaviour of states in other international organizations. Nevertheless, signs of increasing reluctance to live up to their commitments are indicative of the continued efforts that market making will require of them. Effective cooperation between nation states is never easy to achieve. The EU has made significant progress in achieving such cooperation over the single market. As the subsequent chapters illustrate, however, the more it strays from this core project, the more elusive such progress has become.

5

THE BROADER ECONOMY

B uoyed in part by their success in market making, the member states have expanded their collective ambitions well beyond it. Yet, and as argued in chapter 1, international cooperation is not simply a matter of nation states identifying areas where common action would benefit them and then proceeding with it. States are sovereign political actors anxious to maintain control over their own actions, and governments have domestic constituencies to satisfy. Even in the core area of market creation, as we have seen, such considerations can thwart effective action at the European level. When it comes to dealing with broader economic questions, some of far greater political salience than the single market, they take on added importance.

★

Towards the end of the 1990s, a new economic lexicon emerged. Gone were the days when governments intervened massively in economic matters to foster the development of national champions. Instead, the new orthodoxy stressed the need for 'competitiveness' and 'economic reform', by which was usually implied labour market reform and liberalization. The new thinking was adopted by the Union at the European Council meeting of March 2000. The Lisbon summit stated its ambition to make the EU, within ten years, 'the most dynamic and competitive knowledge-based economy in the world, capable of sustained economic growth with more and better jobs and greater economic cohesion'.

The Lisbon Agenda laid out a number of detailed policy goals related to, among other things, employment rates, research and development spending, improving education and training, promotion of information technology and communication technology and the modernization of social models. Two years after its formulation, Wim Kok, the former Dutch Prime Minister, was requested by the 2004 Spring European Council to lead a group of experts in assessing progress to date.

The Kok Report was presented to the Commission and Council in early November 2004. It concluded that little progress had been made in achieving the Lisbon objectives, and adopted a three-pronged strategy for addressing these failures. Kok stressed the need for member state ownership of the process, for the Commission to improve its peer pressure and benchmarking methods, and for EU policies, particularly the budget, to reflect the Lisbon priorities.

Consequently, the process was relaunched. The Commission's mid-term review stressed the need to focus on growth and employment, and the March 2005 European Council concurred.[1] The 'revised Lisbon Process' was to be based on the publication of annual action plans at EU and national levels. The initial array of objectives was reduced to two specific targets: an employment rate of 70 per cent and research and development spending of 3 per cent of GDP.

For all the ambitious targets, however, Lisbon is flawed in several crucial respects, all involving the reluctance of member states to compromise their own perceived interests. The so-called Sapir Report, commissioned by Barroso, mirrored the Kok Report in emphasizing the importance of using EU policies to facilitate achievement of the Lisbon objectives. Foremost among these was the budget.[2] The notion of a larger budget was rejected almost immediately in preliminary negotiations (see below). And even then, Commission proposals made during the 2006 debates on the EU's financial perspective (2007–13), according to which 60–75 per cent of the money allocated to the structural funds should be earmarked for investments with relevance to the Lisbon Strategy, were summarily dismissed. The attitude of the German Minister for the Economy was instructive, as he stressed that it was up to member states to decide what is and is not good for growth.

There is, moreover, little if anything that the Commission can do to encourage reform. The Kok report had, sensibly enough, emphasized the need for national ownership of reforms associated with the Lisbon Agenda. Yet it had also stressed the need for the Commission to play an active role in naming and shaming those unwilling to act on their commitments. Predictably enough, while accepting the former, the European Council rejected the latter. In the words of Jean Pisani-Ferry and André Sapir, and in a pattern familiar from chapter 3, 'the underlying governance model, where the European Commission played the role of a schoolmaster, has been abandoned in favour of one in which it plays the role of coach.'[3] Contrast this with the single market, where the regular publication by the Commission of 'scorecards' detailing member state progress has been a central, highly visible and rather effective element of the Union's strategy.

Governments, therefore, have been free to do largely as they please. Integrated guidelines for growth and jobs adopted by the Council in 2005 illustrated nicely the incoherence that resulted from decentralized policy making – if only by the fact that there were twenty-four of these. Governments, moreover, seem largely to have ignored the guidelines anyway when drafting their national reform programmes, as has the Commission when assessing them.[4] Unsurprisingly, therefore, the plans vary widely, with Germany hardly referring to services (a central element of the Lisbon Agenda), others talking of tax incentives, others still of pension reforms, and so on.

Thus 'the new governance regime [for the Lisbon Agenda]... rests almost exclusively on national action programmes – with little or no benchmarking and little or no EU funding.'[5] A report published in October 2006 reaffirmed the broad conclusions of Kok that failure was the result of national inaction, and particularly reluctance to implement product and labour market reforms.[6] And this is the crux of the matter. For all the verbal attachment to the Lisbon process, political will to carry out the reforms it implies is too often absent, not least in countries like Italy, where the Prodi government depends for its survival on a razor-thin majority including unreformed communists.

In several continental countries, welfare states effectively act to protect those in the job market from those outside it (leading to, for instance, the widespread protests that saw attempts to reform the contract for young people in France aborted in April 2006). 'Insiders', in other words, make up a large proportion of the EU population, enjoying secure jobs, generous social welfare and high levels of public service.[7] Unsurprisingly, they tend to be less than enthusiastic about plans to challenge their privileged status. Which in turn creates problems for politicians aware of the need for reforms to stimulate employment. As the Prime Minister of Luxembourg, Jean-Claude Juncker, put it neatly, European political leaders 'know exactly what to do, but we do not know how to win the next elections once we have done it'.

Little surprise, then, that progress towards meeting the Lisbon targets has remained halting at best. According to 2005 figures, only Finland and Sweden exceeded the target of 3 per cent of GDP for spending on research and development, with Portugal and most of the new entrants spending less than 1 per cent. Denmark, Holland, Sweden and the UK alone had achieved the target of 70 per cent employment rates, while Belgium, Greece, Poland and Spain languished at the other extreme. Under half look set to meet the target by 2010, with forecasters claiming its realization might have to wait until 2018.[8] And of course achieving the various targets is made all the more difficult by problems within the single market, as an October 2006 report by a team at the LSE made clear. Particular causes for concern were the failure to agree on an EU patent and the disappointing outcome of debates over services.[9]

★

Further clear evidence of the reluctance of the member states to embrace (in their actions as opposed to their rhetoric) the priorities laid down in the Lisbon Agenda is provided by the Union's budget.

Controversy and the budget go hand in hand. Furious arguments and frenzied media commentary characterize discussions of its size, its nature and its sources. Yet the budget puts one in mind of Henry Kissinger's dictum that academic arguments are so bitter because the stakes are so low. The US Federal budget for 2008 was around €2.2 trillion, or 20.3 per cent of US GDP, under plans presented by George Bush in February 2007. National budgets in the EU typically amount to 45 per cent or more of national income, while the combined annual spending of member state governments has been estimated at around €4 trillion.[10] In 2003, the EU's budget amounted to €99.7 billion, equivalent to 1 per cent of the member states' combined gross national income (GNI).[11]

The budget is funded through a combination of customs

and levies on imports, a share of VAT receipts and, most importantly, member state payments based on GNI (which make up three quarters of the total). Germany for many years funded the EC through its disproportionate budgetary contribution. There was much truth to the assertion by Uwe Kitzinger (a former EEC official and early academic observer of European integration) that this represented 'a form of delayed war reparations'.[12] As the 1990s drew to a close, however, Berlin proved a less willing paymaster than had Bonn. And the German government was joined by other net contributors in expressing concerns about the size of the budget. In December 2003, as negotiations started over the settlement for 2007–13, the Heads of State and Government of Germany, France, the UK, the Netherlands, Austria and Sweden wrote to the Commission President demanding that spending levels be capped at 1 per cent of EU GNI.

Unsurprisingly, their demands flew in the face of the Commission's own proposals, which called for an increase of some 25 per cent in the size of the budget to around 1.14 per cent of the Union's GNI. The Commission's position was logical enough. The 2004 enlargement had brought a large group of states significantly less wealthy than the EU average into the Union. The steady increase in Union competences required increased funding, as, too, did the kind of focus on the Lisbon priorities called for in successive reports.

Yet the stubborn resistance of the 'contributors' club' won the day. Final agreement was possible only on a sum of around 1.045 per cent of EU GNI, equating to some €862 billion over the 2007–13 period.[13] And even this was possible only because, once again, Germany acted as paymaster, agreeing to give Poland €100 million from funds originally earmarked for eastern Germany. Barroso summed up the disappointment of many with his comment that 'this is a budget for a mini-Europe.' As striking was the bad-tempered nature of the discussions that culminated in the deal. Almost a year of bitter disagreement between the member states had seen insults traded (Barroso accused Britain of acting like the Sheriff of Nottingham in trying to take money from the Central and East European states in order to retain its budget rebate) and threats of vetoes brandished in a most uninspiring display of meanness.

Indeed, the sheer unpleasantness of the exchanges served to persuade some that the current system of appropriations was unsatisfactory and that a more automatic funding mechanism should be introduced. During the course of 2005 and 2006, a series of proposals called for the introduction of an EU tax – whether this be on short-term financial speculation and international air and sea travel, or on SMS and email messages. The Tax Commissioner, László Kovács, has gone on record to say that the Commission will propose such a tax as part of the Commission's budgetary review leading up to 2009. Given what has been said before about tax, and member state sensitivities about it, we can look forward to a debate every bit as bad-tempered as any on the budget itself.

Problems inherent in negotiating the size of the budget are representative of a broader issue. The member states control the budgetary process and the size of the budget is decided in intergovernmental negotiations. It is hardly surprising, therefore, that these debates see net contributors battling the demands of net recipients. Perhaps more insidiously, however, the same logic pervades discussions of the details of the budget itself.

The crucial question about the budget is not what, but, rather, who it is spent on. As one study has put it, the 'main objective of EU spending... is to achieve acceptable net balances rather than agreed policy objectives.'[14] Each member state attempts to secure the largest slice of the pie for itself, whether this be by limiting its contribution or by gaining increased payments.

Unsurprisingly, therefore, EU expenditure is dominated by two explicitly redistributive programmes – Cohesion Policy and the Common Agricultural Policy (CAP). The former was added to the lexicon of integration in the 1980s under the combined impact of the launch of the single market and Mediterranean enlargement. By the time of the 2005 budgetary settlement, cohesion represented 35.7 per cent of the total budget. Yet while couched in the language of 'solidarity', the true rationale for much spending under this heading has been the need to provide compensation to those member states who fear losing out from European integration. Again, and as in so much else the Union does, member state domination of negotiations concerning the use of the funds perhaps made it inevitable that they be turned into a compensatory mechanism.[15]

Thus, the European Regional Development Fund (ERDF)

was created in the early 1970s largely to compensate the
UK for the unfavourable budgetary situation it would face
upon accession. The cohesion funds, set up under the terms
of the Maastricht Treaty, were intended to provide an incentive for the poorer states to put in place policies allowing
them to achieve the convergence criteria for Economic and
Monetary Union. Certainly the all too evident wealth disparities between the EU15 and the new entrants of 2004
have led to a shift in spending towards the latter. Over seven
years from 2006, Poland will receive almost €60 billion in
regional support from the €308 billion structural fund
budget. Yet the EU15 have held on to what they can, ensuring that significant amounts of money still go to their
poorer regions. One EU ambassador, asked about EU 'solidarity', responded , 'What's that?'[16]

The other major area of spending is, of course, the CAP.
This will eat up 43 per cent of spending in the seven-year
period covered by the most recent budgetary agreement.
Discussions in 2005 and 2006 about the new budget for the
Union provided only limited scope for agricultural reform.
France benefits more from the CAP than the UK does from
its famed rebate (in 2003 France got €10 billion in CAP
receipts while UK received €4.5 billion via its rebate).
Unsurprisingly, therefore, President Chirac had conspired
with Chancellor Schroeder to stitch up a deal at the
October 2002 summit that ensured spending on the CAP
was to rise by 1 per cent a year in nominal terms until 2013.

While agricultural spending dominates the budget, two
caveats are in order. First, in the 1970s, it accounted for

some 70 per cent of the total EC budget. Moreover, because the CAP is a common policy, EU spending represents all agricultural spending in the European Union, which is not the case in other sectors, where governments are at liberty to spend what they like on policies where they share competence with the Union.

Yet, for all this, there is no easy way to defend a policy that continues to consume so much of the Union's budget. Actually, there is no easy way of justifying it at all. The stated aims of the CAP are to provide farmers with a reasonable standard of living and consumers with quality food at fair prices, thereby also preserving Europe's rural heritage. To achieve this, the EEC developed a system of guaranteeing minimum prices to producers for their products and providing subsidies for those crops planted. Article 39 of the EEC Treaty, which dealt with the objectives of the CAP, began with the objective of 'ensuring the rational development of agricultural production'. So much for the good intentions. By September 1990, *The Economist* (which should one day conduct a study of university administration) described the CAP as 'the single most idiotic system of mismanagement that the rich western countries have ever devised'.[17]

At the heart of the iniquities inherent in the CAP are the price supports that originally defined it. Their purpose was to ensure minimum prices for agricultural products. Whatever prevailing market conditions, farmers were guaranteed a certain price for their products. The system works via a number of levies that vary according to changing international prices and ensure that imports do not alter prices. This may have been all well and good at a time when agricultural production levels were low (the founding six member states relied on imports to satisfy the demand for food). The problem is that massive technological advances have made the sector far more efficient than in the 1950s; and the CAP system provided strong incentives for higher outputs. Guaranteeing high prices acted as a protection against the economics of supply and demand; whatever the demand for their goods, farmers had an incentive to keep on producing, secure in the knowledge that the EEC would guarantee a certain price for them. The result was huge surpluses – butter mountains, wine lakes and the like – and the dumping of excess production in Third World economies, which were thus prevented from developing indigenous agricultural industries of their own.[18] Closer to home, estimates suggest that the average European family pays €500 per annum more on food because of the minimum prices guaranteed by the CAP – regressive taxation at its finest.

Yet the most damning indictment is that it fails to achieve even its questionable objectives. It is simply not possible to justify the CAP using any of the rationales generally deployed for EU policy competence: efficiency, redistribution or the needs of the single market. For one thing, the agricultural sector is not what it used to be. Even in France, by the turn of the century, less than 3.5 per cent of the population were active in agriculture, which accounted for under 2.5 per cent of GDP. Farmers represent a mere 2 per cent of the European workforce.

The CAP also leaves much to be desired as a means of redistribution. Wealthy member states receive most from a policy which pays the highest subsidies for products mainly found in northern Europe (i.e. in the six founding member states), including beef, sheep, oats, sugar and milk. While price supports in some areas have been reduced to close to world prices, in others, such as sugar, the Union continues to pay producers more than three times the world price. Beef and poultry farmers receive double the world price. Even with the phasing in of direct payments to new members by 2014 (see below), the Central and East European countries will still receive less per hectare and per farmer than old member states.

Moreover, in contrast to the myth that the CAP exists to preserve traditional European farming, the reality is that it disproportionately benefits large, wealthy farmers. As one observer has put it, for 'decades, the French political elite have manipulated images of humble farmers to provide huge subsidies to the agricultural elite – industrial-scale farmers and wealthy landowners'. In France, the vast majority of CAP funding goes to the largest farms: the ten largest French farms each receive an average of €400,000 while those working the smallest farms are provided with a mere €500. One quarter of all CAP payments, in other words, goes to 5 per cent of French farmers – the largest, richest ones.[19] There are, moreover, no ceilings to the system of income supports in place. And, indicatively of the way negotiations in the EU proceed, the British government is among those fighting to preserve large payouts, arguing that the system should reward the most efficient farmers. It certainly rewards the richest. In 2004, the Duke of Westminster, one of the richest men in Britain, received £448,000.

Some reform has been undertaken of this most iniquitous of policies. Budgetary ceilings were introduced in the 1980s to limit runaway expenditure. In 2003, a deal was struck to de-link payments from production and switch some payments from price supports to direct income payments. Once this has been implemented, around 90 per cent of agricultural support should be non-trade distorting. Yet, and herein lies the ultimate irony, effective reform, in the shape of a total switch from price support to income payments, would shift the burden of agricultural support from the consumer to the taxpayer. In other words, it would increase the burden on the EU budget. Proponents of such a move claim it will increase political pressure to reduce subsidies; many farmers oppose income payments for this very reason. Yet any move towards an increase in the Union's budget seems unlikely to say the least.

Given the above, it should come as no surprise that the budget does little to redirect expenditure towards the EU's priorities, and particularly towards the Lisbon priorities. The Sapir Report had branded it a 'historical relic', with agricultural and regional policy spending coming in for particular criticism. It recommended that a reformed budget should include a fund for economic growth (including research), with agricultural spending reduced to just 15 per cent of the overall total. In the event, the budgetary allocation for Lisbon-type programmes – the budget heading is entitled 'competitiveness for growth and employment' – is a mere 8.4 per cent (46 per cent lower than in the Commission's original proposals).

The fact is that the nature of the EU budget makes it a singularly inappropriate tool for addressing the Lisbon concerns. One of these is research and development spending.[20] Yet, as Begg and Heinemann point out, policies which are not predictable in terms of their redistributive impact – such as research funding for which scientists must bid competitively – make up only a tiny share of the EU budget. And this is necessarily the case given that the real (unstated) aim of that budget is to redistribute money between the member states.[21] In other words, while the budget as it stands undeniably fulfils some (limited) useful functions, increasing it is not a way to promote a more competitive Union.

★

If a lack of central authority is a defining feature, and central cause, of the weakness of both the budget and the Lisbon Process, the problems confronting the euro stem from a combination of unparalleled centralization in the monetary field with continued fragmentation of fiscal policy.

Alongside the market, the single currency stands out as the single most obvious achievement of European integration. The euro was introduced on 1 January 2002. As discussed in chapter 2, its creation resulted from the sense of panic engendered by German unification, and the consequent determination of certain political leaders to drive through a project that they saw as a response to the danger of renewed conflict in Europe.

We've also seen that the policy model for the single currency was the Deutschmark. Thus, the Maastricht Treaty placed monetary policy in the hands of an independent central bank. And price stability – in other words controlling inflation – was defined as the central goal of that policy. Under the treaty, the 'primary objective' of the ECB is 'the maintenance of price stability'. While the bank must support the general economic policies of the Community, this must be 'without prejudice to the objective of price stability'. Naturally enough, 'price stability' was nowhere defined, but it was generally taken to mean an annual inflation rate of less than 2 per cent.

In terms of fiscal policy, the Maastricht 'convergence criteria' set the rules for membership of the single currency. In 1997, the Amsterdam European Council codified those for monetary union itself within a 'Stability and Growth Pact' which reflected German insistence that states with excessive fiscal deficits (more than 3 per cent) or debt (not to exceed 60 per cent of GDP) should be penalized. Should a member state be found to be in serious breach of its terms, the Commission was empowered to recommend that the Council take action.

Economists have written numerous abstruse volumes discussing the merits of EMU. This is not the place to go into detail about optimal currency areas or the like. Yet a couple of peculiarities inherent to the undertaking are worth remarking upon. The emphasis on price stability is itself something of a curiosity. While it made perfect sense for the Federal Republic of Germany – a small, very open economy in global terms – it makes far less for the large, relatively closed eurozone. Clearly, keeping inflation low matters if exports make up a huge proportion of GDP; it matters less if they do not. And the timing of the introduction of the euro served merely to highlight the inflexibility of the price stability fetish. Since its inception, the ECB has had to reconcile its treaty-defined mission with the relatively weak performance of the euro area economy – invariably in favour of the former.

While monetary policy arrangements are rigid, those for fiscal policy are largely non-existent. National fiscal policies remain national and the Union has, as we've seen, only a very small budget. All of which calls into question its ability to respond in the event of a serious economic downturn, and particularly of 'asymmetric shocks' that affect some parts of the eurozone more than others. The budget, aside from being inadequate in size, is also uniquely ill-adapted to intervening in the event of poor economic performance in that it is inherently pro-cyclical – it cannot run deficits and its spending ceilings are expressed as a proportion of Community GNI. Even formerly leading proponents of monetary union have been led to concede that, without significant fiscal transfers, the single currency will fail. In other words, without a sizeable central budget that can be used to compensate when some regions are performing worse than others, the strains on the system will become unbearable.[22]

Running an effective monetary policy in the absence of fiscal tools would be difficult enough within a nation state. The problems of doing so in the Union are compounded by the absence of labour mobility, a crucial element of any response to economic crises that affect some regions more than others.[23] And this is leaving to one side the problems confronting the Central Bank in setting rates for a currency area experiencing variable growth.

Indeed, in a triple whammy, not only is the budget limited, not only does the Stability Pact limit member state spending, but the Pact also calls for fines to be imposed on those countries in the most serious fiscal trouble. Hardly a recipe for fiscal stabilisation. Prior to the introduction of the euro, states in such trouble could have devalued their currency in order to improve their competitiveness relative to their partners and hence reinvigorate their economies. But this is no longer an option. The single currency thus creates a situation in which labour market reforms – not too subtle a code for cuts in real wages – appear as the only solution open to governments already facing economic problems and, presumably, resultant electoral punishment.[24]

So much for the economic theory. And theory is the apposite word, in that the member states, no sooner had they signed up to these rules, began to display their contempt for them. It soon became clear that almost every aspect of EMU was contested. The ECB's independence, as we saw in chapter 3, is impressive by any measure. Yet, and particularly once it had become clear that Jean-Claude

Trichet planned to insist on his independence, relations between the bank and the Eurogroup (the Finance Minsters of the Euroland states) deteriorated rapidly. Disputes focused on what many saw as the overly restrictive monetary policies pursued by the bank. Finance Minsters have not been shy about criticizing ECB rate decisions, particularly the four rises that occurred after December 2005; by November 2006, as the bank expressed concern about the inflation outlook, the Austrian Finance Minister, Karl-Heinz Grasser, snapped that 'core inflation is absolutely under control.'

More broadly, some member states – with France in the vanguard – have pressed for 'economic government', meaning formal mechanisms for discussing those aspects of macroeconomic policy (such as employment and growth) not covered by existing arrangements. Early disputes focused on the perceived need for the Bank to consult more with political authorities. The former French Prime Minister Dominique de Villepin asserted that the Bank 'has to remain independent, but there is no reason why it should not take advice or listen to the views of other people'. All of which serves to make one wonder what independence in fact means, particularly as President Sarkozy seems convinced that frequent public beratings of the ECB will serve to influence its decisions.

Trichet himself has stubbornly resisted pressures for more consultation, fiercely defending the principle of ECB independence and refusing to countenance further meetings with political representatives of the eurozone.

Relations between him and Jean-Claude Juncker, Prime Minister of Luxembourg and inaugural chair of the Eurogroup, took on a Laurel and Hardy quality in 2006. Trichet simply did not reply to a letter from Juncker requesting further private meetings to discuss economic and monetary policy. The latter stamped his foot and proclaimed that 'Those who won't talk to me in a small room will hear me via a loudspeaker.' In a strained joint press conference in September 2006, Trichet invited the assembled journalists to look at their euro banknotes and see who had signed them. Juncker countered by saying his agreement to serve another term as Chair of the meetings of Economics and Finance Ministers (ECOFIN) was dependent on the development of a better working relationship with the ECB.

The notion of economic governance also encompasses the need for more effective fiscal policy mechanisms at Union level. Concerns about the functioning of the Union's restrictive fiscal rules surfaced with a vengeance in 2003 when, with delicious irony, Germany, along with France, found itself in breach of the deficit criterion.[25] The Commission, as mandated under the Stability and Growth Pact, recommended that the Council proceed with the excessive deficit procedure. ECOFIN, however, demurred. It rejected the Commission's recommendations to impose sanctions (even the relatively mild measure of placing a sum temporarily in a non-interest-bearing account) and a decision was taken to 'hold the Excessive Deficit Procedure in abeyance'.

Uncomfortable with being seen to ignore rules they had themselves written, the member states set about rewriting them in such a way as to minimize future transgressions. In March 2005, the European Council approved a revised Stability and Growth Pact. Under its terms, the excessive deficit procedure would not be used against a member state experiencing either negative growth or a long period of low growth (under the original pact, this exemption had applied only to cases of a member state experiencing an unheard of negative growth rate of 2 per cent). And in the event of a deficit, the new pact spelled out a series of ready-made fudges, excuses and mitigating factors. These included: potential growth, the economic cycle, the impact of structural reforms, spending on research and development, medium-term budgetary efforts (such as public investment) as well as investment in such worthy enterprises as fostering 'international solidarity' or achieving 'European policy goals'. Thus Germany could finally win a *quid pro quo* for its budgetary contribution, while also claiming unification as a legitimate reason for missing its fiscal targets. Indeed, it is hard to conceive of any item of national expenditure that could not be legitimized, however dubiously, as geared towards 'European policy goals'.

Hardly surprising, then, that the ECB expressed 'serious concern' about the new pact. Hardly surprising, either, that, in June 2006, the Monetary Affairs Commissioner, Joaquín Almunia, reported that member states had not managed to abide even by their new promises. Notable among these was the pledge to use the nascent economic recovery to restore budget balances. An appalled ECB felt compelled to weigh in, announcing it would not accept sovereign debt from fiscal laggards if their credit ratings slipped. With no credible rules left to impose discipline, Finance Minsters in November 2005 warned Hungary that it risked losing its EU regional aid unless it cut its deficit.

While this ongoing pantomime can be quite entertaining, open political opposition to the monetary policy regime has harmful consequences. A contested governance system is not a recipe for the kind of stability the introduction of the euro was intended to ensure. In late 2006, comments by de Villepin about the need for more political influence over the ECB spooked the markets and sent the euro tumbling against the dollar.

The rules governing the single currency are, therefore, not only questionable in nature but also rarely properly applied. They are, moreover, incomplete. Control over those levers of policy that affect the 'real economy' is located at the national level. The experiences of Ireland and the UK suggest that flexible economies may be one key to growth. Liberalization, investment and labour market flexibility in particular have a role to play in this regard. And eurozone countries have proved no more effective at reforming their labour markets than those states that are not members of the single currency. None of them have achieved the flexibility exhibited in Sweden, Denmark and the UK.

Indeed, there is evidence that membership of the euro-zone has served merely to reduce pressures on governments to reform. Italy is a case in point – albeit an extreme one.[26] The country is characterized by a lack of competition across much of the service sector, low investment, an inefficient budgetary process and a relatively inflexible labour market. Yet, because membership of the euro removes the potential for a currency crisis, successive governments have been able to shy away from reform. The result has been decreasing productivity, inflation above the eurozone average and a sharp decline in competitiveness within the eurozone. Italian unit wage costs have risen by 20 per cent relative to those in Germany since 1999, fostering increasing reliance on imports, with the result that the Italian economy barely grew between 1999 and 2005 (cumulative growth in real GDP was a mere 9.1 per cent).

The parlous condition of the Italian economy has led to fevered speculation as to whether the country would actually remain within the eurozone. Simon Tilford, of the Centre for European Reform, put the chances of the country dropping out as high as 40 per cent.[27] Political leaders have not been slow to stick their oars in. Roberto Maroni, a Northern League cabinet minister, declared that Italy should consider bringing back the lira (triggering a fall of the euro against the dollar), while the Prime Minister, Silvio Berlusconi, commented in July 2005 that 'Prodi's euro conned us all.'

Yet although claims that the eurozone is about to self-destruct make for good headlines, they are hardly convincing. For one thing, Italy has a high debt denominated in euros. Withdrawal would lead to a massive increase in debt payments. Nor do other eurozone members have an interest in seeing even a bad pupil like Italy leave the club, given the danger that this will spark some kind of domino effect, with new-found Italian competitiveness placing pressure on other weaker economies, and the markets searching eagerly for the next state to push through the door. In fact, the real danger confronting the euro is not that of a weak economy leaving, but of a strong economy doing so, or failing to join in the first place. A decision on the part of one of the Baltic states not to join – precisely because of the potential impact of high debt levels and fiscal imprudence in the worst-performing economies – would be a far more likely, and extremely damaging signal. Yet given the irresponsibility of certain existing eurozone members when it comes to the rules of the game, who could blame them for so deciding? Indeed, what a wonderful political gesture it would be if Lithuania, so ridiculously denied access to the eurozone, were to decide to do so.

★

The contrast between the market and EU involvement in the broader economy should now have become clear. In the areas both of the budget and of the Lisbon Agenda, the Union remains hamstrung by the domination of its member states. Ambitious rhetoric notwithstanding (there are those who view it as positive that all the member states have at least signed up to the Lisbon Process), progress in achieving practical objectives remains limited at best. And (as discussed in chapter 7), the disjuncture between rhetoric and reality is itself a potential source of concern.

The euro, of course, is a different kettle of fish. EU powers in the monetary policy domain are far from inadequate. Monetary union illustrates different kinds of problem, problems that emerge when the EU acts on the basis of fear and goes too far too fast. The result has been an incomplete monetary union, with fiscal policy remaining within the purview of the member states. Nor, as the fate of the Stability Pact neatly illustrates, is the solution simply to centralize fiscal policy (as some zealots are wont to propose). What the euro illustrates is that there are limits to what member states will tolerate. The fact of the existence of the single currency leaves them with no real option but to persist, but their unwillingness to follow the rules, or respect the independence of the ECB, makes for a less than satisfactory policy regime. There are those, of course, who see the fact of the euro in and of itself as a cause for celebration. These are the people who view the EU as an exciting project rather than as a response to pressing and real policy problems. We should not be surprised, then, if the Union, in those areas where it simply lacks the powers or the authority to act effectively, continues to be unique, yet flawed.

6

BEYOND ECONOMICS

During the 1990s, as we've seen in chapters 2 and 3, the Union began to gain competence in new areas such as foreign and security policy and justice and home affairs. As is the case for economics beyond the market, it faces the problem of reconciling the way it goes about dealing with these issues with the need to achieve effective outcomes. Form serves to limit functionality.

In foreign affairs in particular, EU involvement has spawned high and hopelessly unrealistic expectations. Decisions in foreign policy are made by unanimity between the member states, all of which retain their determination to pursue their own national policies in addition to whatever they do within the EU framework. Hence EU activity will always be more limited than it is in, say, matters pertaining to the market.

Yet while coming nowhere near to matching the exaggerated expectations it has spawned, the Union has become a useful tool for the member states in those domains where cooperation rather than integration under the 'Community method', or via powerful central institutions, is the norm. Successive enlargements in particular have represented something of a triumph. The secret will be to ensure that expectations do not totally outpace capacities. The institutional limits of EU potential must be appreciated.

★

The Union's role in justice and home affairs is that which has expanded most markedly in recent years. The November 2004 Hague programme made freedom, justice, internal security and the prevention of terrorism priorities for the Union for the next five years. Criminal and judicial affairs now make up almost 20 per cent of all Commission proposals.

Just as the recent surge of interest in energy policy has been motivated by a sense of crisis, so, too, has enhanced member state cooperation in the areas of justice and home affairs been the result as much of fear as anything else. Increasing levels of cross-border crime, of organized crime, and of human trafficking (estimates suggest some 100,000 women and children are trafficked across EU borders annually), coupled with renewed fears of terrorism after attacks in the US, London and Madrid, have heightened perceptions of the need for cooperative action.

Developments within Europe have reinforced these trends. The Schengen Agreement, creating an area without internal frontiers (consisting of all member states bar Denmark, the UK, Ireland and the ten accession states of

2004) and which became operational in 1996, has increased fears about the trans-border nature of crime and criminality. In political terms, national leaders have been anxious to counter the threat from the far right, exemplified by the success of Jean Marie Le Pen, leader of the National Front, in progressing beyond the first round of the 2002 French Presidential election. No surprise, then, that a couple of months later the Seville European Council agreed a number of restrictive asylum and immigration measures.

The fights against terrorism and organized crime have revealed both the strengths and the limitations of the EU. On the one hand, harmonization has proved problematic in the extreme. Attempts at the harmonization of national criminal law have been fraught with difficulties, not least owing to the highly politically sensitive nature of the area. Yet some progress has been made. Member states have agreed on common minimum sentences for serious crimes relating to terrorism, sexual exploitation of children, trafficking, fraud, corruption and money laundering. Prior to EU involvement, only seven member states had specific legislation countering terrorism.

While harmonization has proved problematic, mutual recognition has been a more effective approach, the most obvious example being the European Arrest Warrant. Most member states have in place a 'double criminality' requirement. So if country X requests the extradition of a suspect, country Y will comply only if the act is also a crime under Y's laws. The European Arrest Warrant, in force since 2004, limits the reasons for refusing extradition. It also, moreover, lists thirty-two serious offences – ranging from terrorism to illicit drug or weapons trafficking to murder and kidnapping – for which there is no need for double criminality as long as it is punishable by imprisonment for at least three years. Since the Warrant came into force, average extradition times have been reduced from nine months to forty-three days.[1] During its first year, 175 arrests were carried out in UK under it, and some ninety at UK requests in other member states including, notably, a suspect wanted in connection with the attempted 21 July 2005 bombings in London. In September 2005, Hussain Osman, a suspect in the 7/7 bombing, was extradited to London from Rome far more quickly than would have been possible without EU facilitation.

Member states have also enhanced their intergovernmental cooperation, albeit with mixed results. Following the March 2004 Madrid bombing, the Union appointed an anti-terrorism chief, though Gijs de Vries was tasked merely with overseeing the efforts of governments in terms of anti-terror legislation. Not that much of a chief, in fact (he resigned in March 2007). Similarly, Eurojust was charged with assisting national judicial authorities in working together in investigating and prosecuting serious crime. It serves as a mechanism of coordination and an information exchange in the prosecution particularly of terrorism and human trafficking. Composed of 245 senior prosecutors and judges known (instructively) as 'National Members', its case load has expanded enormously since its creation. In 2004 alone, the number of cases involving four or more countries doubled.[2] Alongside Eurojust, a number of other information-sharing and exchange systems have come into being, such as the Schengen Information System (SIS), containing data on all individuals to be refused entry into the Schengen zone. Similarly, Europol, based in The Hague and home to around 500 staff, aims to facilitate information exchange between national law enforcement authorities via European liaison officers seconded from member states as representatives of national law enforcement agencies. Again, this is a matter of coordination rather than integration: Europol officers have no law enforcement powers of their own, and cannot carry out investigations in member state territories.

Immigration is a centrepiece of EU efforts to create an Area of Freedom, Security and Justice. The Hague Programme places a major emphasis on managing migration flows, setting out an agenda to step up the fight against illegal immigration, including in areas of border security, illegal employment, and return and cooperation with third countries. It is estimated that some 400,000 people cross EU borders annually without the necessary travel documents. Two thirds of these take advantage of the poor controls in those member states bordering the Mediterranean. Malta, with a population of only 400,000, currently hosts over 1,000 illegal migrants, while over 11,000 migrants have landed in the Canary Islands – 900 of these in a twenty-four hour period in September 2006.

Given such population movements, member states increasingly perceive a need for common action. In

September 2006, the leaders of the eight Southern European states wrote to the Finnish Presidency, raising their concerns over the scale of illegal immigration. The varying approaches of the member states clearly posed problems. Different definitions of refugee status, for instance, led to a situation in which 84 per cent of refugees from Chechnya were recognized in Austria, 42 per cent in France, 23 per cent in Germany and none in Slovenia.[3] In response to such anomalies, agreement was eventually reached on minimum standards for qualification for refugee status.

In July 2006, the Commission approved the creation of 'rapid border intervention teams' made up of border guards, interpreters and medical staff contributed by the member states. Operations were to be carried out under the direction of the EU agency for external borders management. Frontex, established in Warsaw in June 2005, is, like the institutions outlined above, limited in scope, being restricted to coordination and risk analysis, and having no cross-border enforcement powers. In August 2006, the EU launched immigration patrols, intended to stop illegal immigrants crossing to the Canaries from Africa. The Hera II mission was jointly funded by Spain and the EU budget and involved naval vessels from Italy and Portugal, supported by Italian and Finnish aircraft, in addition to Spanish military vessels already in the area. The previous May, naval and aerial patrol vehicles had been sent along the coasts of the Canaries, Morocco, Mauritania, Senegal and Cape Verde.

Cooperation, therefore, has borne fruits. Yet there remains a tension between the perceived need for it and continued sensitivities about what is a highly sensitive area of public policy. Illustrative of the persistent differences between national approaches, the Interior Minister, and future French President, Nicolas Sarkozy, openly criticized Spanish and Italian policies of mass regularization (Spain had introduced an amnesty programme under which several hundred thousand people living illegally in Spain were able to apply for work and residency permits). Equally, in May 2006, the member states failed to agree on a list of 'safe' countries whose citizens would normally be denied asylum.

As national sensibilities in the Council increasingly frustrated attempts to move the internal security agenda forwards, the Commission called, in May 2006, for the use of Article 42 of the treaty. The so-called *passerelle* clause allows member states to decide, by unanimity, to move police and judicial cooperation in criminal matters within the community pillar and therefore be dealt with by qualified majority voting with the full involvement of the European Parliament.

The advantages of this from the perspective of the Commission were obvious. For one thing, use of the *passerelle* would allow it to take those member states who failed to implement JHA measures to court. By 2006 only five had implemented legislation to combat child pornography and sexual exploitation. Moreover, the Commission contrasted negotiations over the European Arrest Warrant — which had got bogged down in the Council — with the rapid passing of a (first pillar) directive on data retention at the end of 2005.[4]

Yet a debate launched by the Finnish Presidency in September 2006 found only five states voting in favour of resorting to the *passerelle*, while fourteen voted against. The vote underlined the limits to what the member states will tolerate in such a sensitive policy sector. Instructively, a House of Commons committee report stated baldly that use of the *passerelle* would be an issue of 'constitutional importance', and noted acerbically that matters 'such as what is or is not a crime... are currently preserved for Member States because they affect national sovereignty. Speed of decision making is not a sufficient justification for over-riding a Member State's concerns about such matters.'[5]

Constrained by member state reluctance, EU actions have also been shaped by the nature of decision making. The second pillar is dominated by Ministers of the Interior, safe in the 'silo' of the JHA committee, within which consensus exists on the need to keep migrants out and preserve security. Within (most) national governments, such discussions tend to be more balanced, including not only ministers who recognize the need for migrant labour but also law officers who have heard of the notion of human rights. Moreover, given the peculiar institutional arrangements in place in the EU for security matters, ministers can reach decisions unencumbered by the need to secure European Parliament approval, and safe in the knowledge that the Court enjoys only limited purview over their decisions (see chapter 3).

Little wonder, then, that everything within the second

pillar tends to be viewed through the prism of security. Discussions of immigration are invariably linked to concerns about trafficking and Islamic extremism. A May 2004 directive set out not standards but *minimum* standards for qualification as a refugee, prompting UN Europe's director for refugees to point out the danger of setting minima that member states were free to exceed. The Amnesty International annual report of May 2006 was highly critical of the EU's approach to asylum seekers and migrants, referring to the Union's 'failure to acknowledge that it faced a crisis of protection, rather than of asylum'. The Danish Justice Minister, Lene Espersen, responded to pressure to move certain issues to the first pillar by stating that she 'would rather that things take time, and that the citizens are secured in their rights'.

Concerns about rights-related issues and the European Arrest Warrant surfaced in 2005 as the German Federal Constitutional Court found German implementation of legislation flawed on human rights grounds because of the lack of a right to appeal. This had immediate repercussions, as Berlin was unable to extradite Mamoun Darkazanli, a suspect in connection with the Madrid bombings, to Spain. He was subsequently released. While the Arrest Warrant provides for fast-track extraditions, moreover, there is no sign of a corresponding EU-wide system of bail. Meanwhile, because only courts of last resort can refer matters to the ECJ, there is a danger that disadvantaged groups – particularly immigrants – will find themselves discriminated against because of their limited financial resources.

There is something eerily Orwellian about the notion of an 'Area of Freedom, Justice and Security'. Particularly so given the ways in which the lattermost seems to have subsumed the two former. Perhaps the most respected academic observer of the sector has commented that the EU in practice places security above freedom.[6] All of which reveals, again, the dangers inherent in the silos in which member states make policy together. And, particularly, the dangers of the kind of halfway house in which those silos are protected not only from other national ministers, but also from the full glare of scrutiny by parliaments and courts.

★

Of all EU policies, it is perhaps its international dealings that generate most excitement. Breathless predictions of a powerful EU dominating the world stage are now commonplace.[7] Certainly, the achievements of the Union in its international dealings are not to be sniffed at. Yet, like in so many other areas, they require rather more subtle appreciation.

The market provides the basis for much of the Union's international influence. It is because of their relative wealth that the Union and its member states together provide more development aid than any other state. Moreover, institutions like the EU do not simply allow member states better to confront the challenges of globalization. They can also provide the ability to shape its terms. The sheer size of the single market provides the Union with significant influence in international trade negotiations, where it has become the major player, alongside the US.

As ever, the way the Union works is hardly straightforward. The Commission negotiates trade deals on behalf of the member states. Yet it does so on the basis of mandates provided by national capitals. This is often neither an easy nor even-tempered process, given the profound divisions between member states over the issues of free trade and protectionism. Thus, in October 2005, furious rows erupted as the Trade Commissioner, Peter Mandelson, was angrily accused by the French government of exceeding his mandate by offering a cut of some 44 per cent in farm tariffs in response to a US offer to do likewise. Chirac threatened to veto the trade round rather than accept more CAP reform.

Paradoxically, divisions and veto threats may strengthen the Union's negotiating hand. In a detailed and thought-provoking account, Sophie Meunier argues that under certain circumstances – notably when the Union is anxious to preserve the status quo in terms of the international trading regime – a provision for unanimity and a lack of autonomy from the member states actually helps the Commission to achieve its objectives.[8] Yet interstate haggling also inevitably leads to trade-offs that belie the liberal majority view among the member states. Given the insistence of the protectionist few, and the dangers that they may retaliate in other areas if opposed, it is not surprising that the Union has proved all too willing to protect its market from what some perceive as unfair competition. The period between 1991 and 2004 witnessed a 56 per cent increase in anti-dumping measures,[9] while, their banning by the Uruguay GATT round notwithstanding, the EU continues to employ Voluntary Export Restraints.

When successfully deployed, however, the single market can provide significant international bargaining leverage. This is particularly the case when it comes to shaping globalization via the setting of international norms and standards. As a spokesman for Industry Commissioner Günter Verheugen observed, it's 'a huge advantage if you are the one setting the standards, because it is always better to make the policies rather than to follow them'. Thus, the decision to create a single European standard for mobile phones – GSM – has led to its adoption by some fifty non-European countries, creating a massive market that European manufacturers have come to dominate.[10] Similarly, stringent environmental standards will be less damaging to European industries as long as other states, anxious to retain access to the single market, adopt them as well. Certain EU automobile standards are already applied in countries as diverse as Japan, India, South Africa, Australia and China. And in a sign of its growing self-confidence, the Commission in February 2007 produced a paper stating its global ambitions: 'Increasingly the world is looking to Europe and adopts the standards that are set here.'[11]

The relationship between internal and external policies is, in fact, a two-way street. Effective foreign policies are frequently necessary in order to ensure the achievement of internal goals. Reducing greenhouse gas emissions makes little sense if the other major world economies fail to do likewise. The European Council can put out all the declarations it wants on energy policy. Ultimately, however, supply issues will depend on the Union's success in negotiations with suppliers. And dependence on consensus in Council leaves it exposed to blackmail. Attempts to sign an Energy Charter with Russia were thus blocked in November 2006 by a Polish veto based on Warsaw's desire to end a year-long Russian blockade of Polish meat and vegetable exports.

For all the importance of the market as a basis for the Union's global role, attention tends to focus more on its non-economic international dealings. The EU has, in the last decade, begun to play a role in international security. And this is all the more striking in that, since the ill-fated European Defence Community debacle of 1954, defence issues had been effectively kept off the agenda of European integration. All this changed in the late 1990s, however, with the launch of the European Security and Defence Policy (ESDP). Inconceivable only a decade ago, uniformed military officers now stalk the Brussels corridors, and the Union has developed its own security strategy.

It is, perhaps inevitably, all too easy to mock the ESDP. Ambitions have always outstripped achievements when it comes to the Union's world role. One might reasonably have assumed that the lesson would have been learnt in 1991, when Jacques Poos, Luxembourg's Foreign Minster, declared that the outbreak of hostilities in Yugoslavia marked 'the hour of Europe, not the hour of the United

States'.[12] Yet it was not. When, in the autumn of 2001, a spokesman proudly declared the ESDP operational, he was forced, to laughter from the assembled press corps, to admit that this merely meant that the requisite committee system had been put in place. And when, in December that year, an over-eager Belgian Foreign Minister announced that the Union was planning to send a 'multinational force' to Afghanistan, he was publicly reminded by both the British and German governments that it was not an EU force that would be sent.

Yet ESDP is a reality nonetheless. By the end of 2006, four military and ten civilian missions had been launched. The former ranged from the 7,000 troops deployed as Operation Althea to Bosnia, to anything between several dozen and a few hundred in the cases of the Democratic Republic of Congo and Macedonia. The latter are more varied. The EU Monitoring Mission in Aceh (AMM) has, since September 2005, overseen the peace agreement between the Indonesian government and the Free Aceh Movement (GAM) which put an end to thirty years of civil war. Equally important have been two missions to train judges, jurists and penitentiary officers in Georgia and Iraq. A further two have focused on border control in the highly unstable regions between Moldova and Ukraine, Gaza and Egypt. Finally, an increasing EU speciality is the police mission. Personnel have been deployed both to reassure local populations and to provide training for indigenous police forces in Macedonia, Bosnia, the Democratic Republic of Congo and the Palestinian Authority.

Intuitively, one would guess that the Union should play a significant role in international politics After all, it has a population of some 500 million and substantial wealth, and its member states control considerable military forces, backed by annual defence spending of over €160 billion. Uniquely among multilateral international organizations, moreover, the EU has the capacity to deploy the full range of policy instruments, ranging from aid to trade, to diplomacy, to (limited) military capacities. Moreover, as its own security strategy argues, the sheer breadth of the challenges confronting contemporary Europe – ranging from under-development, to ill-health, to the environment, to terrorism, to population movements and military conflict – call for such a wide-ranging approach. An approach, moreover, that seems particularly appealing in contrast to the overly narrow attitude towards international security adopted by the current US administration, expressed in typically forthright and grammatically innovative terms by leading neo-conservative Charles Krauthammer:

> The world's sole superpower has no business
> squandering its resources and diluting its military
> doing police work and hand-holding in places like
> Haiti, Bosnia and Kosovo... Anyone can peacekeep; no
> one can do what we did in Afghanistan. Many nations
> can do police work; only we can drop thousand-pound
> bombs with the precision of a mediaeval archer...
> Peacekeeping is a job for others.[13]

When the Union deploys its various security policy instruments, the results can be genuinely impressive. Stabilization in the Balkans has involved the dangling carrot of eventual EU membership, the provision of grants and loans, as well as police training operations and (limited) military intervention. It is hard to overestimate the significance of all this, not only in terms of restoring and preserving stability in the region, but also in freeing up front-line troops for deployment to active theatres such as Afghanistan. The very nature of these kinds of missions, however, means the Union fails to receive adequate credit for them. 'Civil War Avoided in Macedonia': not a headline one would expect to see even in the *Independent*.

There are, of course, those who set their sights for the Union far higher. Many in Paris had wanted to see the ESDP develop into a significantly more powerful military tool, allowing Europeans to carry out Kosovo-style military interventions alone and even to act as some kind of 'counterweight' to the United States in global politics. That such hopes have been dashed is due, not least, to the reluctance of any European government to spend enough on defence to match them. And what could have made this clearer than the inability of several of their number to summon up even a few hundred combat troops (preferably of the kind deployable to dangerous places and who are allowed to go out at night) for the ongoing conflict in Afghanistan?

Consequently, the scope for an EU military role is limited. Military interventions by the EU alone will remain exceptional, consisting in the main, as one senior British official has put it, of 'getting cats from trees'. Far more common will be those missions dubbed Berlin Plus (after a NATO summit in that city), during which the EU uses NATO command structures under European commanders (and therefore at the discretion of all NATO members) to carry out its missions. The dream of a European military counterweight to the United States remains as distant as ever.

Yet this should not be a cause for concern. The European Union exists not to replace but, rather, to complement its member states – a fact lost on those who like to equate 'EU' and 'Europe'. European states, including member states, can do many things the Union cannot. From this flow several things. First, that one should not expect it to do what they do. If member states want to carry out large-scale military missions, they can and will do so, but generally within NATO. European states possess significant military capabilities. Remember that French and British Special Forces played a critical role in the conflict in the Tora Bora caves in Afghanistan in 2001.

Second, the EU's ability to act will always be crucially dependent on the ability to secure agreement between its member states. If the notion of majority voting in internal security has caused concerns in several national capitals, it has not even been contemplated for international security affairs. Inaction over Iraq was perfectly understandable in this light (and, as it happens, a qualified majority could not have been mustered by either of the two camps that emerged during the crisis). Similarly, during the August 2006 Lebanon crisis, Britain prevented the EU from calling for an immediate ceasefire. The bottom line is that, on matters of international import, member states, and particularly the larger member states, will always reserve the right to act as they please – as did France, Spain and Italy in November 2006 as they launched a surprise Middle East initiative without prior consultation with their partners. The notion that the creation of an (institutionally muddled) EU foreign policy supremo could alter this situation is naive. Who really believes that particularly the larger member states would call this individual prior to dealing with Washington or Beijing?

Finally, the very nature of the Union means it will always, and of necessity, be a complex and hence somewhat cumbersome actor in international politics. Macedonia alone was host to a bewildering variety of EU actors, operating under numerous separate lines of command. The EU Special Representative was, to an extent, a *primus inter pares*, answering directly to the High Representative for Foreign Policy. Alongside him, however, and each with their own chain of command, were the Commission delegation, an independent reconstruction agency, operating out of Thessaloniki, the EU Military Mission operating under its own chain of command via the UN head of mission in Sarajevo and, finally, Operation Concordia, an EU Berlin Plus operation drawing on NATO assets via the Deputy Supreme Allied Commander in Europe.

All of which serves to give the lie to the periodic scare

stories concerning plans to develop a European Army. It has not, however, prevented the emergence of something of a growth industry among an academic community seemingly determined to talk up the Union's 'new' approach to international security. Terms such as 'normative power Europe' have become the order of the day,[14] with some commentators portraying the Union as a kind of multilateral Gandhi bestriding the world for the benefit of mankind.

Such characterizations are not particularly helpful. For one thing, they set the bar far too high, leaving the Union vulnerable to accusations of hypocrisy. Claims that the EU represents a model of law-based international politics sound false to anyone familiar with the fate of the Stability Pact. The former Australian Prime Minister, John Howard, hit out angrily at EU 'hypocrisy' in pushing other states to adopt stringent Kyoto targets when it has proved unable to meet its own. Lessons on human rights ring hollow from a Union more than half of whose member states have been accused by Amnesty International (in a report of May 2006) of failing to protect asylum seekers and the rights of migrants. Moreover, the Union's 'normative' foreign policies only seem to extend so far. Plans for the EU to use Russian pipes to bring in gas from Turkmenistan and Kazakhstan – two of the worst regimes in the world in terms of their human rights records – led a spokeswoman for the head of Foreign Policy, Javier Solana, to acknowledge simply that the 'democratic west consumes energy and the sources of energy are located, to a great extent, in countries that are ruled by dictatorships'. It will be interesting to see how the Union's new policy of engagement towards Central Asia reconciles the desperation of some member states for trade – particularly trade in energy – with the specialism some of these regimes have developed in torture and extra-judicial executions.

Atop a high horse is not the ideal location from which to pursue a foreign policy. Perhaps it works when one profits from a large power imbalance. The US has managed to get away with a sometimes significant discrepancy between its words and its actions because it is so strong. Europe, however, does not enjoy this luxury. The balance of power in world politics is starting to shift. The West now needs good relations with powerful economic players like India. Consequently, Indian opinions now matter. As it becomes economically and politically more assertive, its government and its people will have more choices to make. Choices about where to work, where to study and where to invest. They will be less willing to do so in countries they perceive – rightly or wrongly – as being places where Indians are discriminated against either on television or at the immigration counter. Delhi's reluctance to sign a draft trade agreement with the EU because of human rights 'riders' that the Union had placed in it served notice about its declining patience with being lectured.

The Union has made great strides in its external policies over the last decade or so. However, and in keeping with the extreme opinions concerning the EU as a whole, observers tend to find it hard to accept these policies for what they are. The danger is that often highly effective if somewhat

low-key approaches to international security become devalued under the weight of unhelpful and unrealistic rhetorical
claims.

★

Article 49 of the European Union Treaty states that any
'European State... may apply to become a member of the
Union'. Accordingly, many have, to the point where existing members no longer know either what 'Europe' is, or
whether such applications are to be welcomed. As we have
seen, each successive round of EU expansion alters the
nature of the Union, introducing states with different policy
priorities, of different sizes, whose membership impinges
on the relative influence of existing members. Gone are the
days when a French referendum on British membership
passed almost unnoticed. In more recent times, the French
electorate, denied a poll on the 2004 enlargement, took out
their frustrations by voting (or so they erroneously
believed) against Polish plumbers.

Some existing member states have, in other words, come
to view the prospect of enlargement with increasing alarm.
Erik Jones, of the Johns Hopkins School of Advanced
International Studies, comments that the 2004 'big bang'
enlargement, involving eight Central and East European
states along with Cyprus and Malta, occurred 'because EU
members could not agree on a workable foreign policy
alternative'.[15] Many of their number would have preferred
not to proceed with it. None of them, however, could come

up with another way of underlining the end of the Cold War division of Europe in the face of insistence by the candidates on their right to join. Enlargement, thus, is both an element of EU external policy, and a result of its shortcomings.

This should not, however, be taken to imply ineffectiveness. Quite the contrary. Enlargement is perhaps the most effective aspect of the Union's foreign policy. It is hard to overstate the remarkable and indeed unique influence it wields over applicant states during accession negotiations. Many have commented on the fact that, through the use of 'conditionality' – holding out the prospect of membership in return for reforms – the Union enjoys an unparalleled ability to bring about peaceful 'regime change' in candidate countries.

As so often, however, the Union suffers for its inability to prove a negative. Prevention does not make for good headlines. Yet the absence in post-Cold War Central and Eastern Europe of conflict over disputed borders, of crises over the treatment of sizeable diasporas, of reversion to authoritarianism, or of systematic and large-scale mistreatment of minorities can all be attributed, at least in part, to the Union's deployment of 'conditionality'. All of which without mentioning the fact that the newly liberated countries of Eastern Europe have all adopted market economies. And while that process was, and continues to be, painful, it has been far more effectively managed than the 'shock therapy' imposed on the Soviet Union.

At the heart of the accession process have been the 'Copenhagen criteria' adopted by the European Council in

1993. These specify the requirements for membership: stable institutions to guarantee democracy; the rule of law, human rights and the protection of minorities; the capacity to cope with competitive pressures and market forces within the EU's internal market; and the ability to take on the obligations of membership. Through the long and tortuous negotiations leading to accession in 2004 and 2007, the Commission was responsible for ensuring respect for the criteria and monitoring implementation of the voluminous EU rule book in each of the candidate states.[16]

Enlargement, moreover, is not a one-way street in that it provides significant benefits for the Union itself. Partly, this is through the contribution new members make in bringing their own particular skills, histories and traditions: environmental initiatives have benefited greatly from the influence of the Scandinavian states that joined in 1995; the single market is larger and stronger as a consequence of successive enlargements. Moreover, unstable borders impact directly on the Union. It has been estimated that 70 per cent of the drugs and illicit goods smuggled into the EU are trafficked through the western Balkans. And early indications are of a drop in crime emanating from Poland after that country joined and began to participate in EU Internal Security policies.[17]

In economic terms, a Commission study on the impact of enlargement two years after accession was bullish in its conclusions: 'the fifth enlargement has acted as a catalyst of economic dynamism and modernisation for the European Union, helping the economies of old and new Member

States to better face the challenges of globalization. At the same time, the economic challenges induced by this enlargement have been absorbed quite smoothly, and there is no evidence of disruptive impacts on the product or labour markets.'[18]

Moreover, many of the concerns expressed by member states about recent enlargements have proven to have been misplaced. Transfer payments from the budget have – so to speak – been capped: at 25 per cent of the payments provided for existing member states in the case of agricultural policy and 4 per cent of a recipient's GDP for structural funds. The sums involved, therefore, have been small – a net benefit of only some €235 billion for all the new members over three years, or a paltry 0.1 per cent of EU GDP. The new member states, it is worth recalling, are small – very small in some cases – with a cumulative GDP of around 5 per cent of that of the EU15.

The impact of labour mobility was also a source of concern, as publics have a tendency to link enlargement with an increasing risk of unemployment. Yet studies suggest that labour from the new entrants accounted for a mere 0.4 per cent of the local EU15 labour force in 2005 – a much lower figure than those for immigrants from other EU15 states and especially for the non-EU labour force.[19]

Reality, of course, does not always impinge upon political debate. Rather than shaping a public opinion ready to be shaped,[20] or, heaven forbid, providing leadership, much of Western Europe's political class has tended to hide behind public opinion in expressing doubts about the value of further enlargement. This had an effect upon the enlargements of both 2004 and 2007 (Romania and Bulgaria), with member states deploying myriad derogations, riders and technical objections intended to limit their impacts.

Bulgaria and Romania have acceded to what is in effect a kind of second-class membership. They are strictly monitored and the possibility of sanctions continues to hang over their heads, despite the fact that they are in receipt of their membership cards. Meanwhile, as we have seen, several of the class of 2004 engaged in an increasingly vitriolic fight over plans to postpone their entry into the Schengen borderless zone. At the same time, while they have their suspicions about discrimination related to, for instance, Lithuania's bid to join the euro, their nationals are subjected to explicit discrimination in terms of the restrictions imposed on their ability to work in other member states. The hypocrisy involved in such restrictions is underlined by their ineffectiveness. Germany was among those to impose strict limits. Yet it is still the single most important destination for workers from the new member states. In 2004 and 2005 it issued one million work permits to jobseekers from them.[21] One can only conclude that the restrictions were imposed for political and presentational reasons, disguising what is in fact a need for immigrant labour.

Misconceptions or not, the fact is that attitudes towards enlargement are changing. As ever, the first thing the Union does when confronting a problem is to invent a new piece of jargon for it. The offending term on this occasion is 'absorption capacity', or the ability of the EU to cope with new

members. As things stand, Croatia and Turkey started accession negotiations in October 2005. Two years previously, at
the EU–Balkans Thessaloniki summit, the EU offered membership to the states of the western Balkans, and in late
2005, Macedonia was accepted as a candidate country.

Of all the candidates, it is Croatia that seems most likely
to join in the foreseeable future. Yet while enlargement is
crucial for all aspirant member states, the most important
decisions will concern Turkey. The decision to admit Turkey
as a candidate for membership was 'a measure of last
resort, taken reluctantly, and then repackaged as a historical
opportunity'.[22] If enthusiasm was limited for the 2004
enlargement, it is even more so at the prospect of this predominantly Muslim (albeit secular) state, partly in Europe
but mainly in Asia, with a population of over 60 million
joining the Union.

Consequently, the EU has hesitated, vacillated, and
stalled in its dealings with Ankara. Hardly surprisingly,
negotiations have proved difficult and often bad-tempered.
Turkish reluctance to open its ports to Cypriot ships and to
repeal article 301 of its penal code (whereby people can be
arrested for expressing non-violent opinions) have proved
particularly contentious. The refusal to open ports led to a
suspension of certain parts of the negotiations in late 2006.

I am not for a moment arguing here that the rules governing enlargement should be ignored. Quite the contrary.
The decision to admit a state to candidate status implies its
willingness to adopt the exceedingly lengthy EU rule book
in its entirety. And the EU should insist on this. It should, in

fact, have done so in the cases of Romania and Bulgaria. Instead, we learn that, in both cases, corruption and the inadequate preparation of systems for the disbursement of EU funds were areas of particular concern even after the decision to admit them. Irresponsibly, the target date of 1 January 2007 was set for Bulgarian and Romanian accession, partly in consolation for missing out on that of May 2004. One can only guess what the impact will be on the reputation of the Union if reports of EU corruption and financial mismanagement proliferate as a result. More importantly, the way the 2007 enlargement was carried out will have an impact on other candidate countries.

EU officials continue to act and talk, in their dealings with these candidates, as if the accession process were based solely on the criteria. The events of 2007 imply otherwise. How must the Turks feel, watching the EU bend, break and generally belittle its own rules in a mad dash to complete the 2007 enlargement? Particularly as this is in addition to what many in that country feel to be EU hypocrisy (under pressure from the Greek government) in its dealings with Cyprus. Turkish Cypriots voted for the UN-sponsored and EU-backed Annan plan for the island, while Greek Cypriots rejected it. Nevertheless, the divided island joined the Union, with the *acquis* suspended in the north. Nor has Cyprus been overly anxious to find a negotiated solution to this situation since its accession. Meanwhile, UN and EU promises to provide aid to, and free up trade with, Northern Cyprus have foundered because of the willingness of the Cypriot government to wield its veto in the Council.

Little wonder, then, that some in Ankara talk of 'Huntington criteria' – after the American political scientist and his 'Clash of Civilizations' thesis – as opposed to the Copenhagen criteria. And such suspicions of EU prejudice are merely heightened by some of the language used when discussing the Turkish application. References to culture, to the importance of Christian civilization and so on hardly help propound the notion that Turkey is a genuine candidate engaged in fulfilling technical membership criteria. Giscard d'Estaing, addressing the House of Lords EU committee, stated that there was, in France, 'this diffuse feeling that Europe was going down the wrong road, that it was initially meant to bring together people who were similar, who looked and felt like each other did'.[23] If only Turks looked more French.

The sad fact is that Turkey has become trapped in a pincer movement between concerns about the functioning of the Union after an enlargement few if any were enthusiastic about and posturing domestic politicians. Fears about 'absorption capacity' mean that some member states claim further enlargement must await institutional reforms that proved impossible to secure even prior to the last ones. French and German fears mean that agreement on such reform prior to Turkish accession is unlikely, to say the least, given their desire to have their size recognized in calculations of majorities in the Council, and consequent fear of Turkish influence under such arrangements.

Politics, on the other hand, means that French and Austrian politicians pander to their publics by promising

referenda on any further expansion. It also led French MPs
to propose a law – condemned not only in Ankara and
Brussels but by all those who understand the importance of
history – making it a criminal offence to deny that mass
killings of Armenians in 1915–19 represented 'genocide'.
Meanwhile, overt US support for Turkish accession (for
reasons entirely unconnected with the well-being of the
EU) plays into the hands of those who see enlargement as
a plot to weaken the Union – much as de Gaulle blocked
the first British membership application (in 1963) on the
grounds that Britain would be a 'Trojan Horse' for
American interests.

The prospects for Turkish accession, therefore, look
bleak. Indeed, it is not overly cynical to suggest that many
political leaders within the EU now view an optimal
outcome as one in which Ankara itself, weary of the delays
and hesitations, withdraws its application, thereby saving
the Union from the political crisis that would undoubtedly
attend any rejection of the application. Interestingly, this is
not the position of either Greece or Greek Cyprus, both of
which, despite their scepticism (to put it mildly) about
Turkish membership, appreciate the leverage that the accession process provides them with in their negotiations over
Cyprus.

It is never nice to lead someone on. It is still less so to do
it while discussing their merits and flaws in public. And far,
far less so when imposing on the prospective partner sensitive changes of a kind that would make timorous West
European politicians cringe. Mark Mardell, the BBC's

Europe Editor, commented on the *Today* programme in November 2006 that the reforms being demanded of Turkey were analogous to a pre-accession UK being told to apologize for its behaviour in India, change the way it policed Northern Island, and hand back Gibraltar. 'If only,' think those opposed to UK membership from the start. The impact of all this on Turkey is difficult to predict, but it would be reasonable to expect some degree of resentment with the Union to result from a possible collapse of accession negotiations.

As importantly, the Union itself has much to gain from Turkish membership. Its prospect has already helped underpin far-reaching reforms, including the abolition of the death penalty, while economic reforms have resulted in the reduction of inflation and high growth (at around 6.5 per cent annually). If ever there was a political case for accession it exists for Turkish accession. What better time and what better way to send out a powerful signal via the inclusion of a predominantly Muslim nation into what is seen by some as a white, Western, largely Christian club? Moreover, Turkish membership would significantly strengthen EU foreign and security policies, not least through its close relations with, and crucial strategic location on the fringes of, what will remain one of the most important and potentially unstable regions in the world – it borders Iran, Iraq and Syria.

★

Whatever the outcome of the Turkish accession process, the Union seems to have lost its appetite for enlargement. It therefore needs to find another way of dealing with problems on its borders. Which poses a simple yet tricky question: how to re-create the influence gained over neighbours by dangling the carrot of membership without that carrot?

Early experience suggests not very easily. Take, for example, the 'Barcelona Process'. Launched with North African 'partners' in 1995, it has involved €3 billion annually of EU grants and loans. Halting signs of progress are visible if one looks very hard. The EU regional forum is one of the few locations where Israel sits down to talk with its neighbours. And observers claim that Moroccan family law reforms have been based partly on EU advice.[24] Yet these are small outcomes for so large an investment in such an important region. Perhaps more tellingly, in November 2005, the EU–Euromed (Barcelona Process) tenth-anniversary summit brought together the member states and their ten Mediterranean partners. Yet not one Arab Head of State bothered to attend, choosing instead to send Prime Ministers or Foreign Ministers. More strikingly still, and indicative of the disillusionment setting into the process, the assembled dignitaries could not agree on a declaration.

The most comprehensive approach to dealing with its neighbours that the Union has adopted is its so-called 'neighbourhood policy'. A cynical view that one hears from time to time in Brussels is that the sole purpose of the European Neighbourhood Policy was to provide employment – if not gainful – to those who had worked so hard and for so long on the 2004 enlargement. Hence the ENP as developed in 2004 was originally designed with only the Union's new eastern neighbours in mind. Only subsequently was it extended to cover all the Union's immediate neighbours. At its heart is supposedly an offer of privileged partnerships between the Union and these neighbours in return for reform. Bilateral plans are agreed, setting out an agenda for political and economic reforms. In the words of the Commission, 'the Union's capacity to provide security, stability and sustainable development to its citizens will no longer be distinguishable from its interest in closer cooperation with the neighbours.' This would be based on the development of new relationships, including the possibility of membership or of participation in the internal market.[25]

All of which sounds encouraging enough, but the reality is somewhat more sinister.[26] Not only do many of the plans provide little if anything in the way of new concessions for neighbouring states, but an emphasis on migration places obligations squarely on these latter effectively to act as buffers between the Union and third countries. Emphasis on the Geneva Convention for the protection of refugees seems intended to ensure the application of the safe third-country rule to neighbours and the return of asylum seekers there, rather than to ensure the safety of migrants. Profound traces of the security-obsessed Area of Freedom, Security and Justice can thus be detected. Encouraging neighbours to adopt repressive measures against their own nationals seeking to travel to the EU might well undermine their own authority, while doing so with nationals of third countries might undermine the stability of their region.

The Union still has much thinking to do, therefore, when it comes to dealing with its neighbours and its neighbourhood. Painful decisions await, particularly as regards its eastern neighbours and the eventual limits to enlargement. Drawing lines will not be easy, partly because all prospective candidates enjoy some support in the Council, partly because simply dashing their hopes of eventual membership removes the major source of leverage over them that the Union possesses. On the other hand, acting the serial tease is hardly a long-term strategy, and will become less so if the Union sparks off an anti-Western backlash in a Turkey that feels it has been misled.

★

Institutionally weak it may be, but the Union has accomplished impressive things both in coordinating the actions of its members in dealing with matters related to Justice and Home Affairs, and in building an international presence for itself. Enlargement, meanwhile, has provided the Union with some spectacular success stories.

Clearly there are profound limits to its capabilities in these areas. And, as in the case of monetary policy, integration in haste and on the basis of fear, as has happened particularly in the case of the Area of Freedom, Justice and Security, can lead to ineffective and indeed inappropriate policy outcomes. Effectiveness within limits is perhaps the lesson of this chapter. And necessary limits are a theme which features prominently in the next.

7

THE STATE OF THE UNION

If this book has worked as I had hoped, the issues raised in a somewhat abstract manner in chapter 1 should now have become clearer via the detailed discussions that followed it. So, we can now return, armed with this knowledge, to the themes raised in that initial chapter and to an overall assessment of the European Union.

As we've seen, most assessments of the EU – whether by Eurosceptics who fear it, or Europhiles who expect too much of it – are negative. One reason for this is what academics call a 'category error'. Observers have a marked tendency to use the template of the nation state against which both to judge the Union and to guide their prescriptions for its reform. For its opponents, the Union is coming to resemble a state, and this process should be stopped. For zealots, a federal European state remains the ultimate objective.

Both sides fundamentally misunderstand not only the EU itself, but also the twenty-seven states that make it up. These states, as each of the preceding chapters has underlined, control what the Union does and how it does it. Far from being some kind of state in the making, the Union is a tool of existing states. And it is only by taking account of their role and influence that the state of the European Union today can be understood.

Understood and, indeed, appreciated. For, seen in this light, the Union is not merely a unique but also a highly successful exercise in interstate cooperation. Its nature, however, limits its potential.

★

Assessment of any phenomenon, as I pointed out in the introduction to this book, requires a yardstick against which this can be carried out. Because the EU performs many of the tasks performed by states, it is tempting to use the nation state as a comparator. This temptation has got the better of people for years. The 1950 Schuman declaration, as we saw, made reference to the federal future of European integration. Walter Hallstein, first President of the European Commission, described the EEC as 'a federation in the making'.[1] His nemesis, Charles de Gaulle, was less than convinced:

> Hallstein believes he is the President of the supranational government. He does not even hide his plan, which is to transpose to the European level the institutional structure of federal Germany. The Commission would become the federal Government.

The European Parliament would become what is today
the Bundestag. The Council of Ministers would become
the Bundesrat – that is, the Senate! This is crazy.[2]

Almost fifty years later, it was one of de Gaulle's succes-
sors who took up the theme again. Making full use of the
pulpit afforded him as President of the Convention on the
Future of Europe, Valéry Giscard d'Estaing called for an EU
Declaration of Independence,[3] and appeared to compare his
role with that played by Thomas Jefferson at the 1787
Philadelphia Convention that led to the creation of the
United States.[4]

The nation state analogy has been picked up by commentators and political leaders alike. Yet it is flawed. Not least
because many so-called 'comparisons' are based on, at best,
a somewhat starry-eyed view of the nation state. A leading
academic observer of federalism has remarked that comparisons of the Union are often based on caricature, on the
notion of a state within which 'decisions are made expedi-
tiously, at a high level of regulation, and with full
democratic participation by interest groups and social
forces.'[5] We see this in the outpourings of Eurosceptics
waxing lyrical about the 'mother of all parliaments', by
which they presumably mean the docile, largely ineffective
and party-dominated institution that is the House of
Commons. Nor is the phenomenon confined to the lunatic
fringe. Oxford's Vernon Bogdanor has commented that the
EU was 'founded… on a conception of government that is
outdated in the modern world of participatory and assertive

democracy'.[6] Few observers would recognize this characterization of contemporary political life.

Indeed, many of the most acerbic criticisms directed at the Union could equally well be applied to nation states themselves. Take over-regulation. Not only is EU regulation agreed upon, and often proposed by, the member states themselves (remember carrots as fruit?) but even supposedly liberal states have a marked tendency to over-regulate. The British Chamber of Commerce estimates the annual cost in the UK of regulations introduced since 1997 at over £50 billion. Under British law, you can kill or give away a bullfinch, but you can't sell or barter it.[7]

Comparisons between the Union and member states are thus often a case of pots and kettles. Yet their most troublesome feature is their fundamental misunderstanding of the Union itself. If the preceding chapters have illustrated anything, it is the scale of the influence wielded by the member states over all parts of the EU system. Not only does the Council of Ministers provide a forum for the expression of the interests of national governments that is absent from, say, the federal system of the United States (US State Governors do not participate directly in national politics), but even the supposedly independent institutions are increasingly prey to member state interference.

To emphasize the location of real political power, let's go back for a moment to the earlier discussion of the incentives confronting Commissioners. Prodi, Delors and Louis Michel were all at some point tempted by the prize of high office at home while carrying out their functions in

Brussels. Now imagine the analogous situation in the United States – of George Bush leaving the White House early to become... Governor of Texas.

Power, in other words, resides in the parts. And the centre lacks the resources to challenge them – resources not merely in a budgetary sense, though we've seen that the Union's budget is paltry. More broadly, the Union lacks those powerful tools and symbols of the modern state – police, customs services or armed forces. It even lacks an administrative or legal presence within the member states and is thus heavily reliant on these latter to ensure the implementation of its laws (which, of course, is not always ensured).

Sovereign states are unique political actors, benefiting not only from material resources but also from significant legitimacy at home and under international law. Internationally, it has been a convention of international politics since the 1648 Treaty of Westphalia that sovereign states are accorded certain rights and a certain respect. At home, meanwhile, the nation state has become the prime object of political loyalties. Politics, via political parties, and its representation, via the media, are structured nationally. National communities, bound by history, memory and shared loyalties have proven highly durable and highly individual.[8]

Which is why, for instance, language plays such an important role in the EU. Translation is big business – 1,416,817 pages of text were translated in 2003. The EU must be multilingual because language matters. To take an extreme example, Chirac walked out of the March 2006 European

Council meeting when Ernest-Antoine Seillière, the (French) head of the European employers' union, made a plea for economic reform in English – or what he referred to as the 'language of business'. Language is a fundamental element of the identity of the member states, so most things, and all laws, must continue to be translated into all of them.

Sovereign states also reserve the right to choose the areas in which they cooperate. Consequently, and unlike in 'normal' political systems, they 'pick and mix' their EU involvement. Britain, Denmark and Sweden have opted to remain out of the euro (presumably illegally in the latter-most case, given treaty stipulations that all but the UK and Denmark had to join once having satisfied the convergence criteria). Britain and Ireland secured protocols to the Amsterdam Treaty allowing them to exercise their own frontier controls, and decide, on an *à la carte* basis, in which second pillar initiatives they wish to participate. Similarly, groups of states wanting to do more than their partners have found ways of doing so. In May 2005, Austria, the Benelux states, France, Germany and Spain signed the Treaty of Prüm enabling them to share information on fingerprints and DNA and to cooperate more closely on airline security.

What differentiates the Union from a state, therefore, is the fact that is made up of states. Prescriptive use of the nation state analogy is therefore often misleading. It can also be dangerous, partly through serving as grist to the Eurosceptic mill, partly, too, because it serves to raise expectations unrealistically and proposes inappropriate solutions to misunderstood problems.

Take the idea of employing the term 'constitution' for the recent revision of the EU's founding treaties. Jack Straw displayed staggering naivety in arguing that all 'sorts of organizations which are not states have constitutions – from golf clubs and political parties, to the UN'.⁹ Golf clubs, political parties and the UN, however, are not routinely accused of harbouring superstate ambitions. Nor do golf clubs (I stand to be corrected, having never ventured within one) include within their constitutions provision for a 'Foreign Minister'. As we've seen, the notion of an EU Foreign Minister is not convincing. It is, in fact, all too redolent of the way in which the inclusion in the ECSC Treaty of provisions for a Court and Parliament betrayed the federalist ambitions of its drafters. And so it is hardly surprising that fear of the Union's superstate ambitions was a factor in the Dutch and French referenda. Certainly, following those popular votes, the terms 'constitution' and 'Foreign Minister' were quickly buried and replaced in the – otherwise virtually identical – Reform Treaty.

The EU suffers from our inability to cope with its uniqueness. In the same article, Straw employed another couple of wildly misleading analogies:

the constitution of the world's most complex international organisation – the United Nations – fits easily into my jacket pocket. The constitution of one of the world's oldest and most successful democracies –

the United States – would fit neatly into the other
pocket. I do not have a pocket big enough for what
passes as the constitution – 'the consolidated Treaties'
– of the European Union.

Little wonder. The United Nations Charter is, undeniably, short. It can be, because the UN is a traditional
international organization, controlled by its members, and
particularly by its Security Council. To such an extent that
divisions within the Security Council rendered it almost
wholly ineffective during the Cold War. Conversely, the US
constitution is pithy because its signatories were agreeing to
the creation of a new nation state.

The EU, in contrast, cannot have this kind of short founding document because it is neither a traditional
international organization nor a state. Member states have
given up powers to an extent unknown in other international organizations. At the same time, they are far more
jealous of their prerogatives than states in a normal federation – hence a complex treaty, riddled with riders,
exemptions and exceptions, specifying prerogatives in cor-
uscating detail. Indeed, Straw's Britain has hardly set an
example when it comes to a willingness to compromise in
order to keep the treaties simple. It was Britain that most
strongly supported the introduction of pillars to separate
sensitive issues from the Community institutions; Britain
which secured opt-outs in the form of declarations
appended to (and lengthening) the Treaties on Economic
and Monetary Union and Justice and Home Affairs. Britain

that insists on similar declarations to ensure the Charter of Fundamental Rights will not apply within its borders.

Yet misplaced analogies have an unnerving tendency to underpin proposals for the Union's future. The clearest examples are provided by debates about the so-called 'democratic deficit'. As we have seen, the Commission is frequently attacked for its lack of democratic accountability, to the point where provisions for the election of its President are included in the Lisbon Treaty. Such elections, some argue, would also, handily, solve the problem of low turnout at European Parliament elections. As a consequence, the Union would look more like a 'normal' democracy.

Except it wouldn't. For one thing, while the EU does much of what states do, it does far from everything they do. The issues voters care most about – healthcare, education, law and order, pensions and social security, and taxation – are largely beyond the purview of the Union. Those things it does do – monetary policy, market creation and regulation – tend, unsurprisingly, to leave voters cold.[10] It is, in other words, structurally condemned to inspire apathy.

Moreover, the Union generally handles policies dealt with by non-elected bodies within the member states. No one suggests holding elections for the head of OFCOM. Nor are there serious calls to place the Bank of England back under political control (though, following the Northern Rock crisis in the UK, there are those who wonder if it was ever removed from that control). And legitimacy for the idea of a European market comes from the member states themselves, whose elected leaders have repeatedly and explicitly sanctioned the goal of market creation – a central part of EC treaties since the Treaty of Rome.

In this limited Union, the European Commission is no longer the crusading institution with pretensions to 'lead Europe', or to become some kind of 'European government', that it was during the Delors era. It was Delors's very ambition that made leaders like Margaret Thatcher shy away from the idea of elections for his post – he was irritating enough without a democratic mandate. Without such ambitions, no rationale for elections exists. In fact, given what the Commission does, attempts to provide it with such a mandate would be nonsensical. Regulators are meant to be independent. Moreover, in its role as referee between the member states, the Commission depends on a reputation for impartiality that election would serve merely to undermine.

The notion that the democratic credentials of the Union can be improved by introducing elections for the Commission President is thus both flawed and potentially highly counter-productive. Moreover, the lack of interest in the Union fostered by the national nature of both political parties and the media bodes ill for attempts to re-create national electoral politics at European level. Romano Prodi was misguided to think that, once Europe was made, it would be possible to 'make Europeans'. There is, quite simply, no European people to serve as the basis for 'normal' EU politics.

Yet, conversely, the Union can help resolve what are real legitimacy problems in the member states. At the heart of the dilemma confronting European politicians, outlined in chapter 1, is the fact that the boundaries of effective government rarely coincide with those of legitimate government. In other words, while member states inspire the loyalty of their populations, they are hardly efficient when it comes to providing for them. The Union assists them in so doing, through, for instance, the provision of a larger market and collaboration in the fight against terrorism and organized crime.

It also allows member states to adjust to a world of national polities operating in transnational markets. In particular, by allowing citizens of one member state to interrogate the ECJ about the validity of laws in another, it has managed to introduce a unique sensitivity on the part of national political systems to interests outside their jurisdictions. This is what the Cassis ruling, discussed in chapter 2, was all about. French producers were given the opportunity to question German laws made with the interests of German producers in mind. They thereby benefited both themselves and German consumers. In this way, the EU helps rub away the rough edges of national democracy. Integration involves not the creation of a European state, but the taming of existing states in the context of the creation of a European market.[11]

★

Given the influence member states wield over the Union, it should come as no surprise that they are responsible for many of its problems. Financial mismanagement is a case in point. Every year, as the Court of Auditors refuses to sign off the EU accounts, the media revels in accounts of ubiquitous 'European' fraud. Yet some 80 per cent of EU expenditure is spent in and by the member states themselves. The Commission, as we have seen, lacks the resources to police what goes on in their territories. And those same member states are distinctly unenthusiastic about helping. When, in November 2005, EU Finance Ministers promised a clampdown on waste and fraud in the EU budget, they were quick to reject a Commission suggestion that that they should take collective responsibility for the problem. Similarly, proposals that the member states should disclose the beneficiaries of EU funds were, in 2006, rejected by fourteen of the twenty-five.

Indeed, national financial affairs in general have often been deliberately sheltered from scrutiny. As we've seen, national debt levels were one of the criteria specified under the Stability and Growth Pact. Yet in 2005 it was discovered that Greece had been fiddling the books since 1998 and systematically understating its debt. Similarly, it took whistleblowing by the Hungarian central bank to reveal that that the Hungarian government had been using creative accountancy to understate the size of its deficit (which turned out to be some 2 per cent higher than earlier Commission estimates). Joaquín Almunia, the Monetary Affairs Commissioner, has admitted that he lacks the resources needed to analyse national accounts, particularly as governments appear to be hiring private sector banks to help disguise the scale of their deficits.

Chapter 1 discussed the various incentives that lead national politicians to use and abuse the EU. These phenomena manifest themselves in several different ways. First, political leaders often treat the Union instrumentally, as a tool to achieve domestic political objectives. For Tony Blair, the decision to call a referendum on the Constitutional Treaty represented an attempt to take the European issue off the political agenda prior to European and local elections, thereby depriving the Conservative opposition of a stick with which to beat the government. For Chirac, a referendum represented a means of dividing the French Socialist Party.[12]

'Responsible policy makers,' declared Jorma Ollila, chief executive of Nokia, 'do not make irresponsible decisions.'[13] In one sense he was right. Both Blair and Chirac achieved their objectives. In the world of national politics, it is national politics that matters. The trouble is, of course, that responsible decisions for national politics may be irresponsible from the perspective of the Union. And so, ultimately, it turned out.

Another means of scoring points is simply to attack the EU institutions. A former French Foreign Minister, Philippe Douste-Blazy, gave a lesson in so doing when he declared that:

> Everyone can see that the euro today remains an unfinished project for lack of a seriously co-ordinated economic policy between members of the eurozone. Let us not leave economic and budget policy to the

European Central Bank, let us not leave it just to the
European Commission, to people who are not
elected.[14]

A series of cheap shots. Forget the fact that most countries – including France – have independent central banks.
Forget the fact that France signed up to a treaty stipulating
the need for a central bank. Forget the fact that the
Commission does not make economic policy for members
of the eurozone. Forget the problems involved in electing
the Commission. Simply launch an attack and, perhaps, for
good measure, go on to attack the ECB for the resulting
slide in the euro. This is no way to treat a referee. At least in
the highest echelons of professional football, a player or
manager would be fined (a trivial amount, admittedly) for
such an outburst. In the European Union, political leaders
not only deliver them with impunity, but in the expectation
of scoring easy political points.

Blaming the Union for things over which it has absolutely
no control has become something of an art form. In early
October 2005, Jacques Chirac launched a furious assault on
the Commission for failing to intervene in the case of the
American firm Hewlett-Packard, which had announced
plans to cut over a thousand jobs in France. What the
Commission was meant to do about this was anyone's guess.
As, too, was what Chirac meant almost a year later when, at
the annual meeting of French ambassadors in Paris in
August 2006, he declared that the European reaction to
events that month in the Lebanon exposed the weakness of

a Common Foreign and Security Policy that played no role, and, given member state divisions, could play no role, in the crisis.

The real skill, of course, is to have your cake and eat it, to attack the Union for initiatives one approves of. As *The Economist* put it, 'time and again, Finance Ministers have sidled up to Commissioners and muttered: do strike down this bit of state aid, or that case of fiscal nonsense, because we can't do it ourselves – though you must understand, we'll have to criticise you in public.'[15] Germany has not been shy about playing this game. Negotiators from the Federal Government have been known to vote one way in the Council while making it clear that they favour the other outcome but can't vote for it because of pressure from the states in the German federation.

European integration has increasingly come to be seen as a repository for national political hot potatoes. We saw in chapter 2 how this was increasingly common during the 1990s, as member states, confronted with an ever greater number of challenges to which they had no individual responses, resorted to competence dumping.

The Lisbon Agenda is a contemporary case in point. Its nature 'implies EU involvement in policy domains that primarily belong to the responsibility of member states'.[16] The EU has no competence over employment policy and has no tools of its own with which to address growth, competitiveness, labour markets or pension reforms. Yet this has not prevented it from giving a wholly different impression. Both Delors's 1993 White Paper on Jobs, Growth and

Competitiveness (a populist response to the Danish and French referenda on Maastricht) and the Cologne employment strategy (a counterpart to the move to EMU) were contrived to give the appearance of decisive EU action in an area where it could not act.[17] As George Parker of the *Financial Times* put it, approving a plan to reduce youth unemployment 'is a feat easily achieved in a Brussels office block behind a security cordon'.[18] Delivery, of course, is another matter.

Hardly surprising, then, that the European Commission found EU citizens to have 'similar expectations for the Union as they have for domestic politics and political institutions'.[19] A poll on the Future of Europe published in May 2006 found that more than half the respondents wanted the EU to do more to create and protect jobs and safeguard social security, unaware, no doubt, that it has limited ability to address either issue.

There are those who argue that, for all its shortcomings, the Lisbon Agenda has been a useful exercise in benchmarking, encouraging member states to learn from each other, and placing the issues of growth and competitiveness firmly on the European agenda. Yet I remain far from convinced that its benefits outweigh its costs. Heads of State and Government certainly benefit politically from being able to return from summits declaring that 'we've decided to make Europe competitive.' But if the Union takes the blame for the subsequent failure of a process over which it exerts no control anyway, the net result will be damaging. Apparent responsibility without power will merely increase dissatisfaction with it, reducing the desire and ability of politicians to turn to it to address those problems it actually could help to resolve.

The blame game is a feature of all multilayered political systems. American state and national politicians have long understood the art of getting the other to take the rap for unpopular decisions (as Hurricane Katrina illustrated so clearly). In the EU, however, the costs of such behaviour are potentially far higher. The Union itself has no real means to fight back against national political attack. In the absence of a European media, most political news is national and tends to focus on what national politicians say. The Union itself rarely enjoys a right of reply. Moreover, the Commission must be careful not to irritate political leaders on whom it is so profoundly dependent for all it does.

Nor does the EU benefit from the instinctive loyalty of its population. Ceaseless criticism tends, in a way that simply does not happen in nation states, to spawn existential crises. The very existence of, and rationale for, the British state is not called into question when unpopular measures (the poll tax) or ridiculous schemes (marching young offenders to cash machines) are unveiled. The existence of and rationale for the EU are, however, frequently debated. And the more national politicians criticize it, the more this will be the case. Having ensured their creation was so fragile, the least they could do is handle it with care.

Many of the things for which the EU is criticized, therefore, lie largely outside its control. This state of affairs generally suits national governments pretty well, allowing them to avoid blame for their own mistakes while, of course, taking credit for the Union's achievements. The problems start when the scepticism they themselves have done so much to foster erupts in either negative referendum votes, or the increasing political strength of anti-EU parties.

★

So, states dominate a European Union which has little or no existence independent of them. Whether it be the Commission's attempts to set emissions targets, the Court's doctrine of supremacy, problems with the implementation of the Arrest Warrant, the demise of the Stability Pact, the divisions over Iraq, the often highly distorted arguments about services or the implementation gaps that still characterize the single market, their influence is ubiquitous.

Yet precisely because of this, because the Union is a tool of its constituent member states, because it is necessarily highly constrained by them, its achievements are remarkable. The EU represents a unique, ingenious and highly successful example of institutionalized interstate cooperation. Certainly, there are implementation gaps, yet the wonder is that sovereign nation states ever consent to implement laws with which they may well have disagreed. Equally, while a cynical desire to buy off potential opposition to further integration might have lain behind successive decisions to increase regional aid to the poorer member states, the fact remains that such aid is unique in international politics and represents, at the very least, a powerful symbol of interstate solidarity.

Creating a single market between twenty-seven mixed economies is a massively ambitious undertaking, and progress to date has been impressive. And aside from the market, while necessarily hamstrung by member states anxious to preserve their prerogatives, the Union has made important, if limited, progress in establishing an international role for itself, enhancing cooperation on internal security, and, particularly, addressing environmental concerns. What is remarkable, in other words, is that sovereign states have cooperated to the degree they have, not that this cooperation remains limited.

The Union exists to complement, not to replace, the nation state. It is hardly a coincidence that those areas in which it has proved the most active regulator – environmental policy, consumer protection and gender equality – were all new areas of public policy, relatively free from prior national regulation, thus leaving the way clear for a new political actor. And in foreign policy, as we have seen, the only way to assess what the Union does is precisely as an actor alongside existing national foreign and security policies, rather than one attempting to do what nation states continue to do in the international arena.

Yet an appreciation of the Union's nature, and hence the scale of its achievements to date, should also alert us to the limits of its potential. There is only so much weight an international organization can bear, dependent, as it is, on the active and willing participation of its member states. The question left for us, then, is how to make the EU more effective without simply wishing national politicians were different, or the Union itself were something other than what it is.

Rather than wasting time and effort on schemes based on a model that the Union could and should never hope to emulate, attention should focus on the two real problems that it currently confronts. One concerns the scope of European integration, or competences of the Union. Member states are coming to baulk at EU intrusion into what they consider sensitive areas of national life. They themselves must learn to resist the temptation to simply dump their policy problems into its lap. Particularly the traditionally more 'federalist' member states must recognize that steady increases in EU competence may translate simply into equally steady declines in both its effectiveness and its popularity. As argued in chapter 4, a failure to limit the ability of the supranational institutions to nibble away at the edges of national welfare states could have damaging consequences.

In addition, the Commission must, once and for all, change its attitude towards EU competence. Of course, it is no longer the crusading organization of the Delors period. Yet it sometimes gives the impression that, were it not for member state watchfulness, it would revert to type in pressing for ever more responsibilities to be transferred to the European level. There are still signs Commissioners have not accepted their role as facilitators rather than leaders, managers rather than statesmen. Perhaps if member states began to appoint seasoned civil servants, rather than has-been or, worse, wannabe politicians to the College, Commissioners might start to focus on their jobs rather than on their ambitions.

Continued ambitions were implied in Justice Commissioner Fabio Frattini's (unoriginal) statement that 'Europe is... like a bicycle, either it goes ahead or it falls to the ground.' And the institution remains, as under Delors, underpinned by a craving for popularity. Take Commissioner Redding's crusade to ensure the reduction of mobile phone roaming rates. It was populism, pursued despite opposition both from several of her own colleagues and from national telecoms regulators, who argued that only wholesale charges (those fees operators charge each other) should be regulated, leaving consumer pricing to the market. And hypocritical populism at that. How, if the Commission itself seeks popular approval through the use of price controls, can it credibly hope to dissuade national governments from doing the same when it comes to energy prices?

The quest for populism is not only misplaced but also frequently hamfisted. Little needs to be said about the pathetic attempts in Commission statements to bask in the reflected glory of the football match between Manchester United and a 'European XI' in March 2007 (this despite the fact that club spokesmen seemed to believe that its purpose was to commemorate fifty years of their involvement in European football rather than the anniversary of the signing of the Treaty of Rome). Still less time should be wasted on the

Commission's 'Plan D' (standing for democracy, dialogue and debate) which, unnoticed by the public, was an attempt to draw them into debates on the Union's future. Either national political leaders choose to educate their publics about the Union, or these latter will remain ignorant. But, as we saw in chapter 1, these leaders have few incentives to do so.

Of more serious concern was the decision to create a so-called Globalization Adjustment Fund in December 2006. The €500 million pot was promoted by, among others, the Commission, the French government and certain academics.[20] Yet not only is it inadequate – the trivial sums involved serve merely to emphasize member state responsibility for welfare policies – it is also misplaced. It reinforces the perceived link in the minds of some between the EU and the often painful effects of globalization which result more from governmental action or inaction than from anything the EU itself can do or has done. It is, in other words, a tiny sticking plaster misapplied.

What the EU needs is not a popular Commission, but an effective one. As illustrated in chapter 4, market creation cannot be carried out without effective institutions. Indeed, this was a lesson learnt by those arch marketeers in the Thatcher government:

> A state was needed, to safeguard the order
> spontaneously generated by the market, but a state
> minimal in its functions and limited in its powers.
> Although the state was to be limited, however, it

needed to be strong in carrying out its functions. Policing the market order required vigilance and firm action to enforce laws impartially so that competition might be fair, exchange voluntary and the fruits of enterprise secure.[21]

The key words here are 'limited' and 'strong'. The more the Commission aspires to extend its remit, the more constrained it will become in terms of resources, and the more exposed it will become in terms of national political backlashes. Focusing on core tasks is the rational alternative.

And all the more so in an enlarging EU. Building on Rousseau's stag hunt, David Hume used the analogy of two neighbours who agree to drain a meadow, knowing that neither could do so alone. They can do so because ''tis easy for them to know each others mind'. Equally, however, ''tis difficult, and indeed impossible, that a thousand persons shou'd agree in any such action...' because a thousand people cannot know and trust each other to the same extent. Cooperation becomes more difficult as more participants engage in it. As numbers rise, therefore, the need for effective central institutions, for Hunt Tsars, merely increases. And similar arguments can be made regarding many of the institutions created at European level. Thus the post of counter-terrorism coordinator will never prove a truly effective one unless member states address the issues of its competences and resources (disputes over which, according to some in Brussels, led to the resignation of its first holder, Gijs de Vries in March 2007).

Ultimate responsibility, of course, lies with the member states themselves. The EU is their creation and, for all the treaty stipulations concerning their independence, they control its institutions. The 'competence dumping' of the 1990s that they themselves initiated served, paradoxically, merely to increase their wariness of those institutions. States will always try to influence those institutions they create. They will try to get away with what they can, even while showing rhetorical attachment to the notion of independence. We saw this clearly in the case of the Commission and the various institutions created to oversee monetary union.

As a consequence, efficiency will always be counterbalanced by considerations related to the nature of states. Thus, while national banks can and usually do publish minutes of the meetings where interest rates are set, the ECB does not do so, out of fear that this will encourage member states to place pressure on 'their' people. Institutions in nation states can also appoint staff on merit. In an ideal world, so, too, would the EU, but member state insistence on representation militates against this (as we've seen with both the Commission and the ECB). The Union is thus dependent, for the quality of its staff, on the member states themselves (though it hardly inspires confidence when the incoming head of the Polish Central Bank refers to a former – and subsequently deceased – head of the ECB as one of his future partners).

States will always, therefore, be reluctant to respect the principle of independence. And the bottom line is that there are limits as to how far they accept any role for international institutions – even if they have provided them with this role in the first place. Take this reflection on the ignominious demise of the Stability and Growth Pact in November 2003:

> This event has proven that, whatever sovereignty large countries are willing to cede to the Commission in matters of importance like fiscal policy, they will take it back – legally or less legally if necessary for a sufficient number of them. It is probably more constructive to simply recognise this point of realpolitik, declare the Pact dead, and return fiscal discretion to national governments.[22]

With no control over national fiscal policies, spendthrift member states could free-ride – tolerating inflation because its monetary implications would be shared between all euro members. Yet fiscal policy is so important to national governments that they will, in the last resort, refuse to abide by any rules but those they set themselves. Think back to our Hunt Tsar. The hunters may tolerate him regulating the hunt. Yet they may equally baulk at the idea that he should decide on how they distribute their catch among their children. So, too, will states baulk at the notion of EU intervention under single market legislation serving to erode highly popular elements of national welfare states.

It is too late to learn this lesson for the euro. It is not, however, too late, to learn it for other sectors. Clearly, a rationale exists for enabling more effective decision making on measures relating to police and judicial cooperation in criminal matters. The Commission has resorted to its favourite tactic of scaremongering to make its point. 'Shall we,' asked Barroso in May 2006, 'have another terrorist attack before we have effective common action?' Functional logic, however, is not sufficient. For EU action to be effective, member states must accept, and continue to accept, the need for that action. There is nothing worse for the Union than member states signing up for initiatives they subsequently realize are too important to be dealt with in Brussels.

The reaction of a House of Commons select committee to proposals for using the *passerelle* on matters to do with internal security is instructive in this regard:

> ... there is the question whether it would be acceptable for the European Parliament to have the right of co-decision on measures about police and judicial cooperation in criminal matters when the most of its Members do not represent and are not answerable to the electorate of the UK.[23]

Some things, in other words, can happily be dealt with by a transnational assembly. Some things, however, are just too sensitive to allow for this. Predictably enough, the Liberal MEP Andrew Duff responded furiously, declaring that it 'is an absurd idea that the parliament would have no right to legislate because it has "foreigners" in it'.[24] And, yes, the notion is unattractive, but it is far from absurd. National politicians guard their prerogatives. And the more sensitive these prerogatives, the more they will be inclined to defend them.

Similarly, while opinion polls indicate broad public support for more effective collaboration on cross-border crime, as *The Economist* points out, such findings are not always reliable:

> The claim that public opinion will support 'more Europe'... is untested. Asked if they want the EU to do more in almost any area of public concern, people will tend to say yes. Asked if they want, say, their homes searched at the behest of a foreign judge, they will say no. Opinion polls are of little use when the precise phrasing of a question is this sensitive.[25]

Better, then, to take popular and political sensitivities into account *prior* to any decision to confer responsibilities upon the EU. Integrate in haste, repent at leisure is hardly a good recipe for Union or national capitals alike. And halfway houses, holding areas that, for some, represent a prelude to full-scale Union involvement, can be the worst of all worlds. Again, internal security is illustrative in this regard. On the one hand, use of the *passerelle* would be problematic from the point of view of national sensitivities. On the other, the precarious solution that sees the sector placed in the third pillar not only leaves the Union open to criticism for ineffectiveness, but also has pernicious, not to say reactionary, implications, owing to a lack of parliamentary control and the limited role allowed to judicial authorities.

What the member states must do, therefore, is resist the temptation simply to dump problems they cannot resolve alone on a Union that lacks the legitimacy to help to resolve them collectively. All the more so because there exists no obvious way of 'repatriating' competence from the EU. This too was picked up on in the House of Commons report referred to above. EU parlance generally refers to the *passerelle* as a 'bridge'. The committee, however, preferred the notion of 'gangplank' to emphasize the one way nature of the process. An ability to renationalize policy is likely to become increasingly necessary as sensitivities about EU involvement in high-salience policy sectors becomes more marked. So, too, is the ability to prevent EU institutions expanding the Union's competence through the back door. We saw in chapter 4 that Court judgments in areas such as health and taxation pose significant challenges to member state prerogatives in these areas.

The problem is that it is only via unanimous action that member states can bring about treaty changes limiting EU competence. And it is generally possible to find at least one member state with its own good reasons for preferring the status quo. Ultimately, however, concern about the extent of EU activities can breed frustration with all those activities. If member states are willing to defy the Commission over fiscal policy, it is inevitable that, sooner or later, they will try the same thing over a sensitive piece of single market legislation. If you ask a referee to arbitrate in transfer disputes as well as officiating in matches, his officiating as well as his arbitration will eventually be called into question. Contempt in one area risks bringing disrepute onto the system as a whole. EU intrusion into health care, or taxation, or internal security, serves as grist to the mill for those national politicians only too happy to question the role of the institution *tout court*.

Which brings us back to where we began in chapter 1, to the paradox of integration: the tension between the need for international institutions and the political incentives at the national level not to recognize the fact openly. It is this paradox that lies at the heart of the problems confronting today's European Union.

The member states are, as we have seen, generally only too happy to sign up to ambitious, 'transcendental' declarations. The March 2006 European Council saw no national leader willing openly to defend an energy strategy of fostering national champions protected against foreign takeovers. The resultant declaration, moreover, called for the completion of the internal market for energy by mid-2007 and 'the full, effective and transparent implementation of internal market legislation'. Yet there is frequently a gulf between such rhetoric and the reality of policy. And subsequent policy failures at the European level can be blamed on the Union.

Member states, in other words, wield power without responsibility. And the only solution is to imbue them with a sense of responsibility. There is no point assuming that this will come about out of a sense of duty. Rather, it is necessary to foster a sense of ownership on the part of the member states. They must, therefore, become genuine and open stakeholders in the European integration process. Only then will the incentives for them to treat the EU as cavalierly as they currently do decrease.

The obvious place to start is the Council, and particularly the European Council, where, as illustrated in chapter 3, their dysfunctional role is perhaps most marked. The temptation of the European Council to resort to 'transcendental' discourse has been alluded to on several occasions, and was encapsulated in the ludicrous claims made at the launch of the Lisbon Process. The problem is that Heads of State and Government feel free to assemble, make ambitious declarations, go home, forget about them, and then let the Union take the flak for a lack of delivery. Perhaps if individuals were entrusted in the Council declarations themselves with overseeing such initiatives, this tendency could be reduced. Gordon Brown, for instance, could take responsibility for ensuring that the EU became the world's leading knowledge-based economy in ten years. Or, alternatively, he could prevail upon his partners to effect a welcome toning down of ambition.[26] The point here is not – as implied in the Lisbon Treaty provision for a full-time Chair of the European Council – leadership. It is the need for organic and clear links between the EU and national politics. The conceptual trick lies in seeing the Union not as a replacement for, or duplicate of, the member states, but, rather, as an extension of them.

And obvious national ownership must pervade all levels

of the Council system. The Presidency, for all its faults, helps nurture such ownership in the state holding it (if it is done right). ECOFIN was hugely irresponsible in refusing to sign up to a declaration entrusting its participants with responsibility for EU finances. Similarly in agriculture, because the CAP is no longer an EC common policy in anything but name, full transparency about recipients is a minimum requirement. Eventually, consideration should be given to a move towards co-financing from national budgets, which would automatically implicate national political systems in the process.

Ownership over the Council, however, is not enough. Perhaps the most innovative scheme contained within the Lisbon Treaty is the so-called 'yellow card' procedure. Its purpose is to allow national parliaments to vote on Commission legislative proposals. Should a sufficient number express dissatisfaction, the Commission would have no choice but to withdraw the measure. The 'yellow card' procedure marks a step in the right direction. The creation of an organic link between EU action and national parliamentarians would make it more difficult for these latter to attack the Union with impunity. And if they felt the need to be bitter about the outcome of such votes, their bile should logically (not a guarantee of anything in politics, admittedly) be targeted at their counterparts in other member states, and not the Union itself.

More broadly, and looking ahead, the Union has proved incapable of assuring its own legitimacy via its own elections. If the European Parliament did not exist today, it would not be created. The political mood is far different from the federalist zeal that afflicted some of the architects of the Coal and Steel Community. If member states succeed in limiting the scope of integration, as I've argued they should, the rationale for a separate, European, parliament is weakened anyway. If, on the contrary, issues like internal security move into the first pillar, the EP will have a new reason to justify its existence given the tremendous political sensitivity of the subject.

Yet given the legitimacy problems that beset it and the irresponsibility of many of its members in seeing their role as champions of integration, its existence now should be a matter for debate. National governments clearly do not want such a debate. Whatever their thoughts on the EP, there are just some things politicians cannot say or do. One such thing is to scrap a parliament. However convincing the logic behind such a move, making the arguments would be far too difficult.

Yet they should at least consider making the case. Prior to the introduction of direct elections to the EP in 1979, it was composed of members appointed from national parliaments. At least they enjoyed legitimacy at home. Yet a parliamentary assembly in Brussels (or Strasbourg, for that matter) is simply too remote from the national political scene. The ideal would be to allow for full involvement of national parliaments in EC decision making. The system, after all, couldn't be much slower than it currently is, with the provision for multiple EP readings on Commission legislative proposals. Technology, presumably, could be harnessed to this end. And it would link national politics directly with the Union.

A potential model for the form of partnership advocated here exists in an area where the Commission enjoys unparalleled autonomy. Under regulations passed in 2004, the EU competition regime has been decentralized. National competition authorities are now allowed to apply the relevant EU treaty articles and national courts to hear competition cases under EU law. Not only does this free up Commission resources, but it also allows for a sharing of responsibility, making national institutions complicit in the European integration process, and consequently making it harder for national politicians to abuse that process. Such are the real benefits of effective and open partnership between the European and the national.

★

We need, as I pointed out in the Introduction, to understand the European Union in order to be able to assess it. Given how it works, what it does and what it is, it is clear that national politicians often attempt to make it do things it cannot do. Hence the problems of excessive competence that now bedevil it. I have argued that the Union is a necessary and in many ways highly effective tool of its member states. This is not to say, however, that it should do everything that it does, or that it does everything well. In order to ensure its continued effectiveness, those responsible for its future must recognize that there are limits to what an international institution can accomplish, given the inevitable reservations felt by nation states about seeing their prerogatives eroded. Union and member states must work together in order that the former works at all, thereby enabling the latter themselves to work more effectively.

Conclusion

EUROPE'S UNLOVABLE UNION

Machiavelli advises the Prince to be feared, not loved.
The European Union's resolution for the new half
century should be to give up trying to be loved. The
EU provides real benefits: some are incalculable, like
peace; some are important, like big markets and
competition; some are concrete, like work permits,
travel without passports. But once achieved, they are
taken for granted. People notice only if the lights go
out. So be more modest. Forget the flag, abandon the
anthem. Do amendments, not constitutions. Love is
unlikely; fear is impossible. Let's be boring.[1]

If the preceding pages have illustrated anything, it is that
the fears the European Union engenders are misplaced.
Claims concerning the creation of a European super-
state, or a relentless crushing of national individualism by
a massive, all-powerful and hugely ambitious Brussels
bureaucracy, are the stuff of fairy tales (increasingly indis-
tinguishable from stories in many British newspapers).

Equally pernicious, however, is excessive devotion. The exaggerated ambitions of the federalists are every bit as damaging as the unfounded attacks of the sceptics. All too often, they result merely in excessive ambitions, competence dumping and ultimately ineffectiveness. Yet many observers continue to display a tendency towards impatience with what the Union does do, in favour of grand ambitions about what it potentially could.

It is not hard to understand why the details of European integration have failed to inspire or to enthral. A late nineteenth- and early twentieth-century European history of wars and genocide, alliances and counter-alliances, revolutions and invasions, treaties and Congresses has been replaced by a later twentieth-century 'narrative' of disputes in secretive council chambers about fishing quotas, rape seed prices and qualified majority voting.

Not surprising, then, that sympathetic observers have a tendency to make exaggerated and sexed-up claims. Or, alternatively, to legitimize the Union with reference to an inspiring future, a future often based on its transformation into some kind of state-like entity.

Yet the EU, as we have seen, is not about to become a state-like organization, and no amount of wishing otherwise is going to alter that fact. Indeed, so reliant is the Union on its constituent member states that it is not even necessarily capable of keeping the lights on, as we saw in the discussion of energy policy in chapter 4.

Attempts to talk up the Union or to provide it with the symbols of a political community — be it flag, anthem or whatever – serve merely to distract attention from its real achievements. They also raise unrealistic hopes among Europhiles, and unfounded fears among Eurosceptics. Alternatively, it can lead to sub-optimal outcomes with serious and damaging consequences. The notion that the alternative to the euro was renewed violence between European states was simply fictional. And the rush to monetary union has left us with a single currency disliked by its members, whose rules they routinely ignore, and whose long-term stability, if not sustainability, is open to doubt.

Moreover, grand projects have a tendency to divert attention away from existing ones. What the Union has delivered is a market, made possible by previously unimaginable levels of cooperation between its member states. Yet the single market is far from complete, and acting as if it were will not assist in ensuring the necessary level of political will to secure its completion.

Excessive ambition, what is more, leads to a desire to see the Union expand its scope into areas where the member states are not comfortable to see it go. This, too, is a recipe for a weakening of the system, as national governments baulk at the loss of autonomy implied by such an expansion (as they did with the Stability Pact). One outcome can be the unsatisfactory halfway house, whereby the Union apparently enjoys competence over policies the member states, in reality, control.

Certainly, it would be nice if national politicians were more open and honest about the EU. And doubtless there are those who wish the Union could weaken the hold that

nation states exert over the loyalty of their citizens, if only
to dampen the worst excesses of nationalism. But this is not
how things are. National politicians act according to the
incentives provided by national politics. Nation states are
resilient organizations, commanding the loyalty of their
populations. Acting as if the world were otherwise, possibly
in the hope that doing so will lead it eventually to catch up,
is delusional, not to say dangerous.

Beneath the ambitious rhetoric, the reality of European
integration has remained stubbornly staid. In March 1983,
EC leaders met to celebrate the twenty-fifth anniversary of
the Treaty of Rome. Gaston Thorn, the Commission's
President, declared that the EC found itself threatened by
nationalist and protectionist tendencies, that the 'European
idea' was losing popularity because the Community seemed
unable to resolve the economic crisis. Twenty-five years on,
The Economist, ruminating on the fiftieth birthday of the EC,
referred to the problems of economic crisis and popular
dissatisfaction with the Union, while protectionist tendencies in the member states have been a target of its ire for
some time now. *Plus ça change.*

Another constant of European integration is instability.
The Union is a delicate balancing act between complete
national sovereignty and the creation of a federal state. It is
a curious hybrid, displaying apparent state-like elements
along with features redolent of other international organizations. It serves to help states – ultimate repositories of
political loyalties, yet ultimately unable to provide individ-
ually for their populations – to deal with the ever-increasing

array of transnational policy problems that confront them. Yet history provides few grounds for optimism as to its stability. Writing in the mid-1960s, one of the most perceptive political analysts of our times commented that:

> Between the cooperation of existing nations and the breaking in of a new one there is no middle ground. A federation that succeeds becomes a nation; one that fails leads to secession; halfway attempts like supranational functionalism must either snowball or roll back.[2]

It's worth bearing in mind that these words were written by a Frenchman. And where you stand on the EU depends partly on where you sit within it. It's easier for a German, brought up in the weak, decentralized state that emerged from the Second World War, to understand power sharing at the EU level than it is for a British person accustomed to the massive concentration of power in Westminster. It's more plausible for a francophone Belgian to appreciate how one can share a political system with others without becoming like them than it is for a Frenchman brought up in the Napoleonic tradition of centralization.

Nevertheless, there is still a widespread and palpable sense of the Union being somehow unfinished, a work in progress. How many times do we hear European integration being described as a process or, worse still, a project? The EU does not fit our conceptual boxes, and hence appals our tidy political imaginations. It is redolent of a half-finished jigsaw. It offends our sense of order, the temptation being either to finish it or to clear it away.

Yet the failing is one of political imagination and not of the Union. It is a complex polity designed for a world of complex politics. It tames states, constraining their ability to close their markets to their partners, allowing them to act together in other areas when they so wish. The member states and the European Union together form the outlines of a European political system, with the European level profoundly dependent on the national but helping them, nonetheless, to achieve their objectives. It's a bit like the rules in place to govern European airspace. Controlled up to 28,500 feet by the individual member states, but thereafter jointly managed for all flights crossing Europe.[3]

If the Union did not exist, it would not now be created. War, material devastation, fear, and the unusual status and mindset of the continent's most powerful country combined in the 1940s to create a unique historical moment in which sovereign nation states consented to relinquish a part of their autonomy in order to accomplish something together. Yet it does exist, and the member states would be all the poorer – both literally and metaphorically – without their unlovable Union.

NOTES

INTRODUCTION: EUROPE FOR THE EXASPERATED

1. *The Economist*, 29 May 1997.
2. To explain. The European Economic Community, later renamed the European Community, was created in 1958. Under the Maastricht Treaty, finally ratified in November 1993, the European Union was created. This contains three 'pillars': one dealing with foreign policy and another with internal security and justice matters, and the final one being the EC. So the EC survives, within the EU.
3. C. Patten, *Not Quite the Diplomat*, London, Allen Lane, 2005, p. 34.

I. THE PARADOX OF INTEGRATION

1. J. Dunbabin, *France in the Making, 843–1180*, Oxford, OUP, 1985, p. 277.
2. S. E. Finer, *The History of Government from the Earliest Times: Empires, Monarchies and the Modern State*, Oxford, OUP, 1997, pp. 1623–4.
3. J. Veverka, 'The Growth of Government Expenditure in the United Kingdom since 1790', *Scottish Journal of Political Economy*, 10 February 1963, p. 114.
4. J. Dunn, 'Introduction: Crisis of the Nation State?' *Political Studies*, 42 (1994), p. 12.

5. The MORI Social Research Institute provides longitudinal data on 'priorities' since 1970, and finds that the economy was the number one in the late 1970s, and is now trumped by public services. http://www.mori.com/pubinfo/rd/sri-change.pdf.

6. Finer, *History of Government*, p. 1570.

7. Crispin Black, 'Intelligence Got It Wrong', *Guardian*, 8 July 2005.

8. France 2, 13 September 1999. See also http://solidarite etprogres.online.fr/Editoriaux/Texte9918.html.

9. See *Guardian*, 26 April 2005.

10. E. L. Morse, *Modernization and the Transformation of International Relations*, New York, Free Press, 1976, pp. 82–9.

2. FROM PEACE TO PROSPERITY

1. Perhaps the best account of the historical development of European integration is D. Dinan, *Europe Recast: A History of European Union,* Basingstoke, Palgrave Macmillan, 2004.

2. The most insightful accounts of this early period, on which this section draws extensively, are to be found in the works of Alan Milward. See, for example, *The Reconstruction of Western Europe 1945–51*, London, Methuen, 1984; *The European Rescue of the Nation State*, London, Routledge, 2000.

3. What goes around comes around. Fifty years later, as the EU Ambassadors of the member states met for the first time after the signature of the Amsterdam Treaty, the French Ambassador criticized Chancellor Kohl's reluctance to make concessions during the negotiations in the face of strong resistance from the German states (Länder). His German counterpart replied that 'having insisted on the creation of a weak and decentralized state after the war, you can't now criticize us for having a weak and decentralized state'. Conversation with author.

4. The issue of the location of European institutions is worthy of a book in its own right. The furious rows as the Foreign Ministers competed to have the ECSC institutions located in their own countries foreshadowed years of similar squabbles.

5. Jean Monnet, *Mémoires*, Paris, Fayard, 1976, p. 295.
6. It is interesting to note that France's boycott of the Council effectively brought the institution – and hence the Community – to a standstill. Fifteen years earlier, the members of the UN Security Council took advantage of a Soviet boycott of that institution to vote through a resolution authorizing intervention in Korea. In other words, the unanimity lock in place in the EC is more stringent (as abstentions count as negative votes) than that in the UN.
7. Economists have tried, and failed, to establish a link between the creation of the EC and these economic conditions. Yet it is important to note that, in the minds of many in the original member states, European integration became, from the first, synonymous with economic revival. This stands in stark contrast to the attitudes of those states which joined during the economic calamities of the 1970s.
8. The letter is reproduced in full in *The Times*, 1 October 1977.
9. His own belief in the significance of the Single European Act, however, was manifest in his statement that 'The Single Act means, in a few words, the commitment of implementing simultaneously the great market without frontiers, more economic and social cohesion, a European research and technology policy, the strengthening of the European Monetary System, the beginning of a European social area and significant actions in environment.'
10. Commission of the European Communities, *Completing the Internal Market. White Paper from the Commission to the European Council*, Luxembourg: Office for Official Publications of the European Communities, June 1985.
11. And this despite Margaret Thatcher's prediction that 'in the long term a proud, ancient nation like Spain would baulk at the continued loss of national self-determination in exchange for German-financed subsidies.' Margaret Thatcher, *The Downing Street Years*, New York, Harper Collins, 1973, p. 746. Indeed, Spain was to prove, on numerous subsequent occasions, a

skilled and ruthless negotiator when it came to increasing
payments to the poorer states.

12. Dinan, *Europe Recast*, p. 218

13. This is not to claim that Delors was wrong. The fact is that the
single market provoked a wave of EC legislation aimed at
removing barriers to economic exchange and harmonizing
national laws. It may well be that this represented a large
proportion of the laws adopted in the member states.
Legislative activity of this kind is often hugely technical, and not
of a kind to provoke public or even political attention. Delors's
mistake lay in his decision to draw attention to it in such a way
as to make people worry about his ambitions.

14. Mark A. Pollack, 'The End of Creeping Competence? EU
Policy-Making since Maastricht', *Journal of Common Market
Studies*, 38 (2000), no. 3, pp. 519–38.

15. Address at Catholic University, Louvain, 2 February 1996.

16. Andrew Shonfield, quoted in J. Hayward, 'Institutionally
Inhibited Leadership within Transnational Interdependence', in
J. Hayward (ed.), *Leaderless Europe*, Oxford, OUP, 2008.

17. Article Five of the Maastricht Treaty states that: 'The
Community shall act within the limits of the powers conferred
upon it by this Treaty and of the objectives assigned to it
therein. In areas which do not fall within its exclusive
competence, the Community shall take action, in accordance
with the principle of subsidiarity, only if and in so far as the
objectives of the proposed action cannot be sufficiently
achieved by the Member States and can therefore, by reason of
the scale or effects of the proposed action, be better achieved
by the Community. Any action by the Community shall not
go beyond what is necessary to achieve the objectives of
this Treaty.'

18. For the first time, the Commission lost its traditional monopoly
over policy initiation in the new pillars covering Common
Foreign and Security Policy, and Justice and Home Affairs, and
member states acquired the right to make formal proposals.

19. Elaine Sciolino, 'Summit Fight Shakes Europe', *New York Times*, 19 June 2005.

3. FRAGILE UNION

1. The idea of juxtaposing the two speeches in this way came from William Wallace, 'Rescue or Retreat? The Nation State in Western Europe, 1945–93', *Political Studies* 42 (1994), p. 52.

2. Commission of the European Communities, 'Communication from the Commission to the European Council: The Period of Reflection and Plan D', Brussels, 10 May 2006, COM(2006) 212.

3. Paul Magnette, *What is the European Union? Nature and Prospects*, Basingstoke, Palgrave Macmillan, 2005, p. 38.

4. L. Siedentop, *Democracy in Europe*, London, Allen Lane, 2000, p. 104.

5. The best short introduction to the institutional system of the EU is provided by Hussein Kassim, 'The Institutions of the European Union', in C. Hay and A. Menon (eds), *European Politics*, Oxford, OUP, 2007.

6. 'Many view Mr Delors' efforts to block a deal [with the Americans over agriculture] less charitably, putting them down to his ambitions for the French Presidency.' 'Blood is Thicker than Rape Oil', *The Economist*, 14 November 1992.

7. Édouard Balladur, former French Prime Minister, evidence to the House of Lords EU committee, 23 October 2006, in House of Lords European Union Committee, 53rd report of session 2005–6, *The Further Enlargement of the EU: Threat or Opportunity?*, House of Lords, 23 November 2006, p. 153.

8. As Commissioner Günter Verheugen put it, 'Many people still have the concept of Europe that the more rules you produce, the more Europe you have.'

9. E. Stein, 'Lawyers, Judges, and the Making of a Transnational Constitution', *American Journal of International Law*, 75 (1981), pp. 1ff.

10. Magnette, *What is the European Union?*, p. 139.

11. *Financial Times*, 19 April 2006.

12. Charlemagne, 'Those Ozymandian Moments', *The Economist*, 11 June 2005.

13. ibid.

14. ibid.

15. Raphael Minder, 'MEPs Cool on Call to Attend More Votes', *Financial Times*, 9 March 2006.

16. Magnette, *What is the European Union?*, p. 79.

17. House of Lords EU Committee, *Further Enlargement of the EU*, p. 35.

18. Cited in *EUObserver*, 19 July 2006.

19. The terminology is complex because the reality is messy. Some states are represented at these meetings by their Head of State (such as the French President), others by the Head of Government (the British Prime Minister).

20. Quoted in D. Dinan, *Europe Recast: A History of European Integration*, Basingstoke, Palgrave, 2004, p. 210.

21. Walter Hallstein, 'The EEC Commission: A New Factor in International Life', *International and Comparative Law Quarterly* 14 (1965), pp. 730, 732.

22. European Commission, *Update on the Internal Market*, February 2005, available at http://ec.europa.eu/internal_market/smn/smn36/p30_en.htm.

23. Jeremy Richardson, 'Water', in H. Kassim and A. Menon (eds), *The European Union and National Industrial Policy*, London, Routledge, 1996, p. 168.

24. E. Rieger, 'Agricultural Policy', in H. Wallace, W. Wallace and M. A. Pollack (eds), *Policy-Making in the European Union*, Oxford, OUP, 2005, p. 174.

25. Emile Noël, 'The Permanent Representatives Committee and the Deepening of the Communities', *Government and Opposition*, 6 (1971), p. 424.

26. Magnette, *What is the European Union?*, p. 116.

27. P. Ludlow, 'European Commission', in R. O. Keohane and S. Hoffmann (eds) *The New European Community. Decisionmaking and Institutional Change*, Boulder, Westview Press, 1991, p. 122.

4. MAKING THE MARKET

1. F. Fukuyama, 'The End of History?' *The National Interest*, 16 (1989), p. 8.
2. House of Lords European Union Committee, 53rd report of session 2005–6, *The Further Enlargement of the EU: Threat or Opportunity?*, House of Lords, 23 November 2006, p. 153.
3. Paolo Cecchini, *The European Challenge*, 1992, London, Wildwood, 1988.
4. European Commission, 'Economic Evaluation of the Internal Market', *European Economy*, 1996, no 4.
5. European Commission, *The Internal Market: Ten Years without Frontiers*, 2002, available at http://europa.eu.int/comm/internal_market/10years/docs/workingdoc/workingdoc_en.pdf.
6. The fear of excessive regulation lay behind Margaret Thatcher's declaration in Bruges that 'We have not successfully rolled back the frontiers of the state in Britain, only to see them re-imposed at a European level.'
7. European Commission, 'Second Biennial Report on the Application of the Principle of Mutual Recognition in the Single Market,' COM (2002) 419 final.
8. 'Communication from the Commission to the Council, the European Parliament, the European Economic and Social Committee and the Committee of the Regions: Second Implementation Report of the Internal Market Strategy 2003–2006' COM (2005) 11 final, p. 8.
9. For an excellent discussion, see David Vogel, *Trading Up: Consumer and Environmental Regulation in a Global Economy*, Cambridge, Mass., Harvard University Press, 1997.

10. See R. D. Kelemen and A. Menon 'The Politics of EC Regulation', in Stephen Weatherill (ed.), *Better Regulation*, Oxford, Hart Publishing, 2007.

11. S. Liebfried, 'Social Policy: Left to the Judges and the Markets?', in H. Wallace, W. Wallace and M. A. Pollack (eds) *Policy-Making in the European Union*, Oxford, OUP, 2005, pp. 250–3.

12. ibid., p. 248.

13. Cited in N. Colchester and D. Buchan, *Europe Relaunched: Truths and Illusions on the Way to 1992*, London, Hutchinson Books, 1990, p. 146.

14. Stephen Wilks, 'Competition Policy: Challenge and Reform', in Wallace et al. (eds.) *Policy-Making in the European Union*, p. 116.

15. ibid., p. 125.

16. ibid., p. 128.

17. 'Communication from the Commission to the Council', p. 4.

18. Juan Delgado, 'Single Market Trails Home Bias', Bruegel policy brief 2006/5, October 2006.

19. The existence of discrete national retail banking systems matters because it means that the 'monetary transmission mechanism', meaning the way changes in interest rates have an impact on economies, differs between member states as a function of factors including long- and short-term interest rates, and the number of fixed or variable rate mortgages.

20. European Commission, *Internal Market*, p. 11.

21. 'Communication from the Commission to the Council', p. 16.

22. The debate about services has been a long-running one. Margaret Thatcher in fact had arrived at the Fontainebleau summit of 1984 armed not only with arguments about Britain's budgetary contribution, but also with a paper entitled 'Europe: The Future', calling for the creation of a genuine common market for both goods and services. The paper is reproduced in the *Journal of Common Market Studies*, 23, 1 (September 1984), pp. 74–81.

23. 'Communication from the Commission to the Council', p. 7.

24. Charlemagne, 'Not Yet Free to Serve', *The Economist*, 18 February 2006.

25. While labour costs in 2003 were still much lower in Central and Eastern than in Western Europe (ranging from 12 per cent EU15 average in Latvia, to 53 per cent in Slovakia), and although there has been some relocation of economic activity eastwards, much of this has been by firms facing growing global pressure. Thus at stake was not a choice between remaining in Western Europe or relocating east, but, rather, relocation or facing losing market share and hence shedding jobs. According to one study, 60 per cent of those German companies with investments in Eastern Europe had managed to preserve or create jobs at home.

26. Commission of the European Communities, *An Energy Policy for Europe*, Communication from the Commission to the European Council and the European Parliament, Brussels, COM (2007) final, p. 3.

27. Charlemagne, 'Energetic Debate', *The Economist*, 11 March 2006. The situation in energy supply varies widely between member states. Thus, in the UK, out of the six major players in the energy market, three are foreign-owned (Npower and Powergen are German-owned, while EDF Energy is a French company). The French market, on the other hand, is largely closed – EDF controls 86 per cent of it, while being the second-biggest energy company in Britain, the second-largest electricity and third-largest gas firm in Italy, and overall number three in Germany. See *The Economist*, 11 February 2006.

28. The companies involved also lobbied heavily, resting their case on the market-based argument that they need pipeline assets on their books in order to secure good credit ratings and raise cheap capital for investment on the international money markets.

29. Commission of the European Communities, *An Energy Policy for Europe*.

30. Under the terms of the Kyoto Agreement, the EU had agreed to a reduction of 8 per cent by 2012.
31. *Financial Times*, 23 November 2006.
32. Cited in *EUObserver*, 6 February 2007.
33. *Financial Times*, 12 September 2006.
34. *Financial Times*, 25 September 2005.

5. THE BROADER ECONOMY

1. Commission of the European Communities, *Working Together for Growth and Jobs: A New Start for the Lisbon Strategy*, COM(2005) 24.
2. A. Sapir, *An Agenda for a Growing Europe*, Oxford, OUP, 2004.
3. Jean Pisani-Ferry and André Sapir, 'Last Exit to Lisbon', Bruegel, Brussels, March 2006, p. 1.
4. ibid., pp. 10–12.
5. ibid., p. 6.
6. Centre for Economic Performance, *Boosting Innovation and Productivity Growth in Europe: The Hope and Realities of the EU's 'Lisbon Agenda'*, London, London School of Economics and Political Science, October 2006.
7. John Kay, 'Europe Will Never Vote for Reform', *Financial Times*, 17 April 2006; see also Wolfgang Munchau, *Das Ende der Sozialen Marktwirtschaft*, Munich, Hanser-Verlag, 2006.
8. See *EUObserver*, 6 November 2006.
9. Centre for Economic Performance, *Boosting Innovation*.
10. *The Economist*, 24 December 2005.
11. Figures for the EU budget tend to be given as a proportion of EU GNI rather than GDP. GNI comprises the total value of goods and services produced within a country (GDP), together with income received from other countries less payments made to other countries.
12. Uwe Kitzinger, *Diplomacy and Persuasion*, London, Thames and Hudson, 1973, p. 98.
13. According to Foreign Office figures, the UK is sill the second-highest contributor after Germany even taking the rebate into

account; the FCO claims that the UK contribution net of the rebate and receipts was €3.75 billion in 2003, as compared with €1.73 billion for France and €2.92 billion for the Netherlands. The figures for the period 1984–2003 reveal that Germany far outstripped its partners in terms of its generosity, paying €167.82 billion, as opposed to €57.91 billion for the UK and €28.6 billion for France. During the same period, Spain received €75.98 billion and Ireland €34.35 billion.

14. Iain Begg and Friedrich Heinemann, 'New Budget, Old Dilemmas', Centre for European Reform Briefing Note, 22 February 2006, p. 5.
15. D. Allen, 'Cohesion and the Structural Funds: Competing Pressures for Reform?', in H. Wallace, W. Wallace and M. A. Pollack (eds), *Policy-Making in the European Union*, Oxford, OUP, 2005.
16. George Parker, 'Funding Feud Displays Inertia and Shrunken Ambitions', *Financial Times*, 12 December 2005.
17. 29 September 1990.
18. John Peet, 'The EU Budget: A Way Forward', Centre for European Reform Policy Brief, September 2005.
19. Richard Baldwin, 'The "Non" Was Also against the CAP', Centre for European Policy Studies, Brussels, June 2005.
20. A Commission report from 2005 pointed out that the Union is not competitive enough as a location for research. Commission of the European Communities, Communication from the Commission: *Implementing the Community Lisbon Programme: A Policy Framework to Strengthen EU Manufacturing – towards a More Integrated Approach for Industrial Policy*, Brussels, 5 October 2005, COM(2005) 474 final, p. 5. The DTI's International R and D scorecard, published in October of the same year, showed an increase in R and D corporate investment of 2 per cent in Europe, as compared with 7 per cent in the US and Asia. The innovation scorecard unveiled by the Commission in January 2006 found that only four member states – Sweden,

Finland, Denmark and Germany – could compete with the US
and Japan in innovative abilities.

21. Begg and Heinemann, 'New Budget, Old Dilemmas', p. 5.

22. Paul De Grauwe, 'What Have We Learnt about Monetary
Integration since the Maastricht Treaty?', *Journal of Common
Market Studies*, 44, no. 4, November 2006, pp. 711–30.

23. A European Commission paper published in 2002 and entitled
'Free Movement of Workers: Achieving the Full Benefits and
Potential' reported that, in that year, less than 0.1 per cent of
the eurozone population moved permanently to another
eurozone state – the equivalent figure for the US was 2.5 per
cent.

24. A recent paper by a distinguished economist suggests that the
current fetish for labour market reforms is not necessarily a
solution to Europe's unemployment problems. See James K.
Galbraith, *Maastricht 2042 and the Fate of Europe: Towards
Convergence and Full Employment*, Bonn, Friedrich Ebert Stiftung,
March 2007.

25. Germany in fact breached the terms of the pact for four
successive years. One of the reasons was that it could not
control public spending effectively because of the fiscal rights
the individual German states (Länder) enjoy under the
constitution. *Die Zeit* reported in February 2002 that the Länder
tripled their deficits in 2001 to €28 billion, whereas the federal
government deficit had increased only slightly to €27.6 billion.

26. The following paragraphs draw heavily on Simon Tilford, *Will
the Eurozone Crack?*, Centre for European Reform, September
2006.

27. ibid.; see also D. Gros, T. Mayer and A. Ubide, *EMU at Risk*,
Centre for European Policy Studies, Brussels, 2005.

6. BEYOND ECONOMICS

1. Hugo Brady and Mónica Roma, 'Let Justice be Done: Punishing
Crime in the EU', Centre for European Reform Policy Brief,
April 2006, p. 2.

2. ibid., p. 3.
3. *EUObserver*, 10 October 2006.
4. European Commission, *Implementing the Hague Programme: The Way Forward,* Brussels, Memo/06/254, 28 June 2006.
5. House of Commons European Scrutiny Committee, *Implementing the Hague Programme on Justice and Home Affairs*, Forty–First Report of Session 2005–6, paras 39, 53.
6. J. Monar, 'Cooperation in the Justice and Home Affairs Domain: Characteristics, Constraints and Progress', *European Integration*, 28, no. 5 (2006), pp. 495–509.
7. See, for instance, S. Haseler, *Super-State: The New Europe and Its Challenge to America*, London, I. B. Tauris, 2004; M. Leanard, *Why Europe Will Run the 21st Century*, London, Fourth Estate, 2005; M. McCormick, *The European Superpower*, London, Palgrave Macmillan, 2007.
8. Sophie Meunier, *Trading Voices: The European Union in International Commercial Negotiations*, Princeton, Princeton University Press, 2005.
9. Patrick A. Messerlin, 'A European Economic Agenda after the NO Votes', 35th Wincott Lecture, 3 October 2005, available at http://gem.sciences-po.fr/content/publications/pdf/AWincottMesserlin.pdf.
10. T. R. Reid, *The United States of Europe: From the Euro to Eurovision – the Superpower Nobody Talks About*, London, Penguin, 2004, pp. 126–7. The Commission estimated in November 2007 that some 2.5 billion mobile phone users worldwide use the GSM standard.
11. Cited in 'EU Wants Rest of World to Adopt Its Rules', *Financial Times*, 18 February 2007.
12. *Los Angeles Times*, 29 June 1991.
13. Charles Krauthammer, 'We Don't Peacekeep', *Washington Post*, 18 December 2001.
14. For the original statement, see I. Manners, 'Normative Power Europe: A Contradiction in Terms?', *Journal of Common Market Studies*, 40, no. 2, June 2002, pp. 235–58.

15. See Erik Jones, 'Mis-selling Europe', *The World Today*, January 2006.
16. The Union arguably enjoys more leverage over prospective than actual members. The Romanian Justice Minister, Monica Macovei, stated that 'while we were nearing the date of accession and being certain of this date, the anti-corruption measures were more and more unwanted and criticized.' One can only assume, therefore, that anti-corruption initiatives will slow given that Rumania has now joined (*EUObserver*, 8 January 2007).
17. House of Lords European Union Committee, 53rd report of session 2005–6, *The Further Enlargement of the EU: Threat or Opportunity?*, House of Lords, 23 November 2006, p. 60.
18. European Commission, Bureau of European Policy Advisors and the Directorate-General for Economic and Financial Affairs, 'Enlargement, Two Years After – an Economic Success', *European Economy Occasional Papers*, no 24, May 2006.
19. House of Lords European Union Committee, *Further Enlargement of the EU*, p. 29.
20. A recent report underlined the fact that public attitudes are far from fixed, and hence open to be shifted by political leaders willing to stress the benefits of enlargement. See House of Lords European Union Committee, *Further Enlargement of the EU*, chapter 2.
21. House of Lords European Union Committee, *Further Enlargement of the EU*, p. 29.
22. See Jones, 'Mis-selling Europe'.
23. House of Lords European Union Committee, *Further Enlargement of the EU*, p. 147.
24. Charlemagne, 'Barcelona Dreams', *The Economist*, 26 November 2005.
25. European Commission, 'Communication on the Wider Europe', COM 2003, 104 final, pp. 3, 5.
26. The following is based on Guild Elspeth, 'What Is a Neighbour? Examining the EU Neighbourhood Policy from the Perspective

of Movement of Persons', 10 June 2005, available at
http://www.libertysecurity.org/article270.html.

7. THE STATE OF THE UNION

1. 'The European Economic Community', *Political Science Quarterly*, 78, no. 2 (June 1963), p. 168.
2. Quoted in Alain Peyrefitte, *C'était de Gaulle*, vol. 2, Paris, Éditions de Fallois/Fayard, 1997, p. 286.
3. *European Voice*, vol. 9, no. 13, 3 April 2003.
4. *New York Times*, 15 June 2003.
5. A. M. Sbragia, 'Territory, Representation, and Policy Outcome: The United States and the European Union Compared', in C. K. Ansell and G. D. Palma (eds), *Restructuring Territoriality: Europe and the United States Compared*, Cambridge, CUP, 2004, p. 206.
6. Vernon Bogdanor, 'Legitimacy, Accountability and Democracy in the European Union', Federal Trust Report, January 2007, p. 19.
7. Ross Clark, *How to Label a Goat: The Silly Rules and Regulations that Are Strangling Britain*, Petersfield, Harriman House.
8. To get a sense of the small, yet profound, differences between the various member states, pick up a copy of Trivial Pursuit the next time you visit one. I have particularly unpleasant memories of an evening with French friends watching them discuss alpine skiing, and French cinema of the 1950s.
9. Jack Straw, 'A Constitution for Europe', *The Economist*, 11 October 2002.
10. A. Moravcsik, 'Is There a "Democratic Deficit" in World Politics? A Framework for Analysis', *Government and Opposition*, 39, no. 2 (2004), p. 360.
11. I'd like to thank Stephen Weatherill for opening my eyes to this aspect of European integration.
12. In an interesting reversal of history, Blair's decision put pressure on Chirac to hold his own poll. Some thirty years previously,

the French had held a referendum on UK accession, placing
enormous pressure on Wilson to do the same.

13. *Financial Times*, 22 March 2006.
14. ibid., 30 August 2005.
15. Charlemagne, 'Don't Just Bash the Bureaucrats', *The Economist*,
    15 October 2005.
16. Jean Pisani-Ferry and André Sapir, 'Last Exit to Lisbon', Bruegel
    Policy Brief, Brussels, March 2006.
17. See Erik Jones, 'Mis-selling Europe', *The World Today*, January
    2006.
18. *Financial Times*, 23 March 2006.
19. Commission of the European Communities, *European
    Governance: A White Paper*, COM (2001) 428 final, Brussels, 25
    July 2001, p. 32.
20. Loukas Tsoukalis, 'Why We Need a Globalisation Adjustment
    Fund', discussion paper prepared for the UK Presidency,
    October 2005, available at http://www.number-10.gov.uk/
    output/Page8381.asp.
21. Andrew Gamble, *The Free Economy and the Strong State: The Politics
    of Thatcherism*, Basingstoke, Macmillan, 1994, p. 37.
22. A. Alesina, and R. Perotti, 'The European Union: A Politically
    Incorrect View', *Journal of Economic Perspectives*, 18, no. 4
    (2004).
23. House of Commons European Scrutiny Committee,
    Implementing the Hague Programme on Justice and Home Affairs,
    Forty–first report of session 2005–06, para 50.
24. *EUObserver*, 7 December 2006.
25. Charlemagne, 'Justice by Majority', *The Economist*, 8 June
    2006.
26. For more proposals on how to reform the European Council,
    see David Harrison, 'Time to Shake Up the European Council',
    CER Bulletin, 52, February/March 2007.

CONCLUSION: EUROPE'S UNLOVABLE UNION

1. Robert Cooper, 'One Idea', *European Union: The Next Fifty Years*, FT Business, March 2007, p. 163.
2. Stanley Hoffmann, 'Obstinate or Obsolete? The Fate of the Nation State and the Case of Western Europe', *Daedalus*, 95 (1966), pp. 909–10.
3. I am grateful to Martin Staniland for giving me the idea for this analogy and correcting my numbers.

INDEX

Bush, George W., 158, 215
butter prices, 28–9

Cabinet Office, 18
Cadbury Schweppes, 149
Callaghan, James, 50, 57
Canary Islands, 182–3
Cape Verde, 183
car emissions, 108, 118, 144–5
carbon prices, 142
Cardiff summit and process, 140
Cassis de Dijon, 46, 49, 115–16, 222
central banks, 18, 55, 102, 225
Central European states, 58, 91, 130, 199
    and agriculture, 165
    EU accession, 63, 65, 198
    and EU budget, 160
    gas supplies, 133
Centre for European Reform, 175
Charter of Fundamental Rights, 119, 220
Chechnya, 183
checks and balances, 23
Cheysson, Claude, 74
children, sexual exploitation of, 180, 184
China, 189
Chinese imports, 89, 93
Chirac, Jacques, 63, 91, 102, 129, 162, 188, 216, 224–5

chocolate, 115
Christian civilisation, 205
civil service, 11, 18, 79
COAL, 31, 33–8
Cockfield, Lord, 52, 74
Cohesion Policy, 53, 161
Cold War, 32, 35, 40, 219
    end of, 58, 199
College of Europe, 70, 232
Cologne employment strategy, 227
comitology, 4, 71, 97
Commissioner for External Relations, 105
committee meetings, boycott of, 2
Common Agricultural Policy (CAP), 103–4, 161–6, 188, 242
Common External Tariff, 44
Common Foreign and Security Policy (CFSP), 60–1, 85, 105, 226
Community method, 4, 71, 95, 100, 110, 178–9
competence dumping, 58, 235, 244
competition policy, 18, 121–5
conditionality, 199
Constitutional Treaty, 67, 89–90, 224
consumer protection, 118–19, 230
Convention on the Future of

national debts, 11, 174, 223
National Front, 180
National Health Service, 150
NATO, 38, 194–5
net contributors' club, 64, 159
Netherlands, 44
    and economic reforms, 157
    and energy, 136
    and EU budget, 64, 159
    European elections in, 86
    and mergers, 147
    referenda, 67–8, 85–6, 90, 218
NewYork Times, 68
Nice summit, 63, 66, 75
Nice Treaty, 88, 120
Nokia, 224
North Africa, 208
Northern Ireland, 207
Northern Rock crisis, 220
Norway, 54
nuclear power, 145

OFCOM, 220
oil crises, 40, 48–9
Ollila, Jorma, 224
one-stop shops, 128, 130
Open Method of
Coordination, 104
Operation Althea, 191
Operation Concordia, 195
opticians, 128
Organization for Economic
Cooperation and Development
(OECD), 15, 125

Ortoli, François-Xavier, 41
Osman, Hussain, 181

packaging, 119
Palestinian Authority, 191
Paris, 130, 225
Paris summit, 42, 132
Parker, George, 227
parliaments, national, 84
Patents directive, 146, 158
Patten, Chris, 5
pay, 119
peace, 32–3, 43
peacekeeping, 192
pensions, 83, 156, 220, 226
Philadelphia Convention, 214
Piebalgs, Andris, 145
Pisani-Ferry, Jean, 156
Plan D, 233
plumbers, 130, 148, 198
Poland, 24, 90–1
    central bank, 235
    and economic reforms, 157
    and energy, 136, 138, 190
    and environment, 143
    EU accession, 63, 200
    and EU budget, 160, 162
    and mergers, 147
police, 105, 184, 191, 193, 237
political parties, 4, 216, 218
politicians
    American, 228
    electoral interests, 18–19, 77

and Middle East initiative,
195
and Treaty of Prüm, 217
Stability and Growth Pact,
119, 143, 172, 223, 249
    collapse of, 90, 177, 196,
    229, 236
    penalties under, 168, 170
    revised, 173
stagflation, 48
Stalin, Josef, 37
state aid, 49–50, 57, 121–2,
124, 226
states, federal, 4
steel, 31, 33, 35–7
Strasbourg, 36, 84, 86, 93, 243
Straw, Jack, 218–19
structural funds, 53, 76, 162,
201
subsidiarity, 61, 71
Suez, 123, 135, 148
sugar, 119, 165
Sun headline, 57
supranationalism, 4, 41, 71
Sutherland, Peter, 122
Sweden
    economy, 157, 174
    EU accession, 54, 63
    and EU budget, 64, 159
    and euro, 217
    and healthcare, 150
Syria, 207

takeovers, *see* mergers and
acquisitions

tariff reductions, 43, 49
taxation, 82, 149–50, 156,
220, 239–40
    European, 160
technology, 12, 118, 243
telecommunications, 12–13,
114, 154
television, 197
tennis coaches, 130
terrorism, 23, 179–81, 192,
222, 234, 237
textiles, 48
Thatcher, Margaret, 25, 48,
51–2, 74, 221, 233
    Bruges speech, 56, 70, 72,
    152
The Hague, 62, 182
Thessaloniki, 195
Third World states, 16, 164
Thorn, Gaston, 250
ThyssenKrupp, 123
Tilford, Simon, 175
Tora Bora caves, 194
tour guides, 128
trade, 2, 12, 20, 28, 49, 188,
197
    free, 74, 93, 188
    intra-EU, 114, 117, 125
trade unions, 27
trafficking, 180, 186
    drugs, 181
    human, 179, 181
    weapons, 181
transcendental discourse, 29,
37, 42, 241